STRATEGY FOR ENERGY CONSERVATION IN INDIA

About the Editors

Pradeep Chaturvedi, is a well known Expert in the Energy Conservation and Renewable Energy Sector. His expertise lies in project planning, implementation and management with emphasis on technology transfer and skill building. A number of pioneering projects and studies of national and international significance have been conducted under his guidance. He has planned, developed and implemented projects in the Asia-Pacific region. At present, Mr. Chaturvedi is also working as a Consultant to FAO's Regional Wood Energy Development Programme for Asia.

Mr. Chaturvedi is the Vice Chairman of the World Renewable Energy Network supported by UNESCO and based in U.K. Being a founder of the Bio Energy Society of India, and now its Vice President, he is involved in projecting the bio fuels issue at national and international level.

Mr. Chaturvedi is a Graduate in Engineering. He is a Fellow of the Institution of Engineers (India) and the Recipient of FAO's World Food Day Medal 1991.

Mr. Chaturvedi has edited and authored 16 books related to sustainable development, renewable energy and energy conservation: and has contributed papers at a number of national and international conferences.

Dr. Shalini Joshi is a Project Officer at the Rajiv Gandhi Institute for Contemporary Studies.

STRATEGY FOR ENERGY CONSERVATION IN INDIA

Edited by
PRADEEP CHATURVEDI
Chairman, Technical Committee
The Institution of Engineers (India)

and

SHALINI JOSHI
Project Officer
Rajiv Gandhi Institute for
Contemporary Studies

Published for
RAJIV GANDHI INSTITUTE FOR CONTEMPORARY STUDIES
and
THE INSTITUTION OF ENGINEERS (INDIA)
by
CONCEPT PUBLISHING COMPANY, NEW DELHI

(Proceedings of the National Workshop on Energy Conservation held during 8-9th September 1995 at New Delhi)

RGICS Project: No 13

ISBN 81-7022-643-0

Published and Printed by

Ashok K. Mittal
CONCEPT PUBLISHING COMPANY
A/15-16, Commercial Block, Mohan Garden,
NEW DELHI - 110059 (India)
Phones: 5554042, 5504042

FOREWORD

India desperately needs to increase its power availability to meet its growing energy demand. By the year 2007, India would need an additional power capacity of 147,000 MW and a corresponding investment of approximately US $ 200 billion. Public investment suffers from severe constraint of resources. Private participation and foreign investment are still very limited. Even if all this could be stepped up, there is little doubt that India's electric power sector could gain substantially from the implementation of energy conservation programmes. Unfortunately, out of a budgetary allocation of Rs. 1000 crores in the Eighth Five Year plan for the period 1992-97, for achieving conservatioin equivalent of 5000 MW installed, only Rs. 15 crores were utilized till the middle of 1995! A variety of technical, policy, institutional and information related barriers hinder measures for efficiency.

Recognising the vital importance of energy conservation, Rajiv Gandhi Institute for Contemporary Studies, in collaboration with The Institution of Engineers (India), organised a two day National Workshop on Energy Conservation on Sept. 8-9, 1995. The Workshop brought together for deliberation policy makers, energy experts and practitioners from industry; energy producer and user sectors; and R&D sector. Various aspects related to energy conservation including policy matters, institutional issues, legal framework, and financial incentives were discussed. The participants unanimously recommended an Action Plan consisting of short, medium and long term measures; starting from good house-keeping, requiring little effort in terms of technology and finances, to systems calling for major technological interventions and high capital investments. To achieve all this, a combination of legislative measures and financial incentives will be necessary. It was suggested that a non-statutory authority be set up to go into all the issues and prepare an action plan for legislative and administrative measures.

This volume is a collection of all the presentations made by various experts during the course of the Workshop. We hope that this volume will serve as a good reference material for planning energy conservation in India.

New Delhi
May 1996.

(V. RAMACHANDRAN)
Director
Rajiv Gandhi Institute
for Contemporary Studies

PREFACE

Energy conservation has been recognised as a national priority for over 10 years now. However, concrete steps for achieving energy conservation have been sporadic, halting and lacking in perspective, and determination.

With the high growth and demand for all forms of energy averaging nearly 10 per cent per year and wholly inadequate production of domestic sources of primary energy, the dependence on imported primary energy in the form of petroleum, natural gas and even coal is increasing at a very fast pace and will, in the next few years, become a major burden on the foreign exchange reserves of the country. By the end of the 9th Plan, the import bill on energy is likely to be around $ 20 billion.

In this context the potential for energy saving from determined and well structured efforts is estimated at about 20-25 per cent of our total energy consumption now. While a great deal remains to be done, it should be mentioned that the Petroleum Conservation Research Association has done commendable work in bringing about saving and conservation of pertoleum products. Not much has further been done in the consumption of other forms of energy The recent increase in the prices of the coal and petroleum products will come as a further incentive for energy conservation.

The first step towards energy conservation should be the setting up of a statutory Energy Conservation Authority (ECA) which should be autonomous nd endowed with adequate powers to conduct energy audits in various industrial units, hold consultations with industries and producers of energy and lay down standards for energy conservation and time limit for meeting them. The Authority should also have the powers to consult experts and lay down standards for industrial equipment and home appliances as part of demand side management. The Authority should also have powers for levying penalties and offering incentives for ensuring compliances with established norms and standards. The Energy Conservation Authority should consist of 3 full time members and should have a panel of energy consultants and energy auditors whose services can be availed of from time to time.

Initial funding of ECA should come by way of the Government grant to form the initial corpus and subsequent funding requirements can be made by levying fees on energy consuming industries.

In this compilation a number of papers have been presented by experts who have provided valuable information and thrown up many useful ideas. It is to be hoped that the authorities concerned will utilise these ideas and suggestions and take urgent steps to set up a statutory Energy Conservation Authority.

Organisers of the Seminar, Rajiv Gandhi Institute for Contemporary Studies, Rajiv Gandhi Foundation and Institution of Engineers (India), should be complimented on this laudable effort.

(G.V. Ramakrishna)
Member (Energy), Planning Commission

CONTENTS

ROLE OF INDUSTRY ASSOCIATIONS

ROLE OF R&D AND ENERGY AUDIT INSTITUTIONS

INTRODUCTION

The Institution of Engineers (India) collaborated with Rajiv Gandhi Institute for Contemporary Studies—Rajiv Gandhi Foundation, to organise a National Workshop on Energy Conservation at New Delhi on September 8 and 9, 1995.

The genesis of organising this National Workshop rested with the International Conference on Energy which was organised by the Institution of Engineers (India) as the Indian Member Committee of World Energy Council (IMC-WEC), a year back on 17-18 November 1994, at New Delhi. The conference had brought into sharp focus an urgent need to promote measures for energy conservation in India, and highlighted the complementary and significant role of energy conservation in augmenting the Energy Supply System.

The National Workshop on Energy Conservation provided the requisite continuity and directed concerted attention on all related aspects of conservation of energy. The intensive high level deliberations of experts facilitated emergence of significant recommendations on specific engineering inputs which can play crucial role in development and successful implementation of short term, medium term and long term targeted Plan of Action. A proposal to setup a non-statutory Authority to formulate effective legislative measures and financial incentives for speedy developmemt and implementation of conservation programmes also received favourable support.

IMC-WEC had the privilege to present and discuss the Report of National Workshop at the 16th International Congress of World Energy Council at Tokyo during October 1995. While endorsing the views expressed in the report, the WEC Congress emphasized that the solicited actions should be fully in tune with the on-going trends as observed since the Madrid Congress held in 1992, particularly with reference to the thrust on enhancement of efficiency in production and use of energy. The WEC Congress also suggested partnership between government and entrepreneurs to create economic, legal and commercial framework to facilitate flow of international capital and technology, and strongly advocated acceleration of energy efficiency through technological development with greater inputs into R&D.

It was quite heartening for IMC-WEC, and the Institution of Engineers (India), to find that the expert views of the National Workshop on Energy Conservation were in perfect synchronisation with the international thinking and evoked substantial appreciation and support at the 16th International Congress of the World Energy Council.

I hope this publication, containing papers presented and recommendations made at the National Workshop on Energy Conservation, will serve as a useful document for further action and reference.

N.C. Vaish
President
The Institution of Engineers (India)

New Delhi
May, 1996.

OVERVIEW PAPERS

ONE

ENERGY CONSERVATION PERSPECTIVES FOR INDIA

PRADEEP CHATURVEDI and M.P. NARAYANAN

As per 1991 census, India's population was 844 million as on March 1, 1991. About 26 per cent of the population lives in urban areas. The population of the four metropolitan cities of Delhi, Bombay, Calcutta and Madras account for nearly 4.6 per cent of the total population of the country. The population is estimated to cross the 930 million mark by the end of the current year.

Indian economy continues to be primarily based on agriculture even though its share in the GDP at constant prices has been declining over time. The share of agriculture sector in the GDP has declined from 39.7 per cent in 1970 to 29.5 per cent in 1993 whereas that of the industries sector has gone up from 17.4 per cent to 22 per cent during the same period. The average rate of growth in GDP, which was around 3.5 in the 70s, has averaged more than 5.6 per cent during the 80s. This trend in GDP growth is likely to continue in future.

The coefficient of elasticity of final commercial energy consumption with respect to GDP at constant prices has been 1.14 during the period 1970-1993. The elasticity coefficients for coal, electricity and refined petroleum products for the corresponding period are 0.54, 1.82 and 1.43 respectively.

As far as energy intensity of the economy is concerned, the primary commercial energy intensity has increased from 1841 KJ/ Rupee (at constant prices) in 1970 to 2445 KJ/Rupee in 1993 whereas the final commercial energy intensity has increased from

1411 KJ/Rupee to 1605 KJ/Rupee during the same period.

Energy Conservation Efforts in India

The Government of India took a few major energy conservation initiatives as listed in Annexure I. The fiscal measures adopted are listed in Annexure II.

The Advisory Board on Energy in February 1983 recommended setting up of a well structured and funded energy conservation organisation as early as possible to act as a nodal point in the Central Government for matters relating to energy conservation. The Advisory Board on Energy, through its high powered structure had created a significant impact on the need for energy conservation. Also the Chairman of the Advisory Board, being an eminent person, carried weight with the government and could deal directly at the highest possible level.

The Inter-Ministerial Working Group Report 1983 has made a series of recommendations on the organisational infrastructure required to support a comprehensive energy conservation programme.

The government founded the Energy Conservation Cell in the Department of Power, with the responsibility of carrying out energy conservation activities. The government also appointed an Adviser (Energy Conservation) in the Cabinet Secretariat, who became a nodal point for the energy conservation activity from June 1990.

The Department of Power in 1989 established the Energy Management Centre (EMC), an autonomous organisation, to assist in an energy conservation programme with the foreign assistance from the EEC, World Bank, UNDP and other agencies.

Following are some selected efforts initiated by various organisations:

National Productivity Council

The National Productivity Council was the pioneer in energy auditing of the industrial sector. Two hundred industrial units covering 12 sectors indicated a potential for saving energy upto 25 per cent in the industrial sector. An estimate was also made that an investment of

Rs. 51,400 million in energy conservation scheme would save a capital expenditure of Rs. 79,800 million on energy production besides reducing energy costs of the consuming sectors by avoiding a recurring annual energy bill of Rs. 37,190 million. A follow-up study by NPC in 1985 of 178 units in 12 sectors covered in the earlier study revealed that 70 units (40%) had implemented energy conservation programme successfully, while 29 units (16%) were yet to start energy conservation programme. The pace of implementation has generally been slow and the energy savings achieved were Rs. 102 million per annum against a theoretical potential of Rs. 830 million, indicating that 12.3 per cent of the saving potential has been achieved in these units.

As a component of the Indian Power Sector Assessment Study, conducted by the National Productivity Council in 1991, under the World Bank and bilateral donor agencies, it was estimated that 20 per cent saving in demand projections are technically cost effective. The estimate based on the potential and applicability of the 27 energy conservation opportunities, such as high efficiency motors, compact fluorescent lamps etc., can realise capital cost of Rs. 43,000 to Rs. 69,000 crores depending on the low cost and high cost scenario projected by the CEA in India Power Sector by 2004-05. This would mean a reduction in peak demand of about 38,000 MW and 61,000 MW respectively. Technologies for the energy efficiency equipment, products and processes have to be developed or technology transferred or imported to realise this potential.

Federation of Indian Chambers of Commerce & Industries

Another survey by the Federation of Indian Chambers of Commerce

TABLE 1.1: **Energy Saving Achieved By Respondents**

	No. of Units	% of total Respondents
Upto 5%	128	37.54
5 - 10%	72	21.11
10 - 15%	34	9.97
15 and above	43	12.81

and Industries (FICCI) in 1988, carried out in 341 units, revealed that several industries were able to realise savings as shown in Table 1.1.

Within the country itself one perceives wide variations in energy consumption within a sub sector, for example in the steel sector, the consumption varies from 8.7 - 15 G Cal/tonne of crude steel. The figure for developed countries is 4-6 G Cal/tonne of crude steel. The energy consumption trends in SAIL plants indicate a lowering in

TABLE 1.2: **Energy Consumption in SAIL Plants**

Year	Energy Consumption G Cal/tonne Crude Steel
1984	11.2
1987-88	10.7
1989-90	10.2

consumption with advancing years (See Table 1.2).

FICCI had subsequently carried out a number of other similar studies for other sub sectors of industry.

Associated Chambers of Commerce & Industries

Associated Chambers of Commerce and Industries (ASSOCHAM) in 1991 covered the sub sectors of chemicals, cement, engineering, automobiles, polymers and rubbers, metals, textiles, leather and food industries. The study revealed that in general, large industries were found to be well organised and well informed in energy audit subsidy schemes and equipment financing for energy conservation schemes. Such awareness was not generally evident with medium and small scale industries. Several of the industrial units had undertaken energy audit with professional assistance from outside consultants. The percentage share of energy cost in the total cost varied from a low of 0.36 per cent in Farm Equipment Limited to as high as 65 per cent in Chemplast.

Following variations in terms of cost for energy consumption were observed:

Engineering industry (including automobile) 0.36-2.1%

Cement	21-36%
Plastics	6.00-30.96%
Textiles	0.33-10.4%
Metals	3.34-7.3%

Shortfall in Energy Production Targets

The energy scene in the country is one of grave concern. Plan projections for additional power generation capacities have not been met due to lack of foreign financial investments and in-country private sector investments. The expected additional power generation capacity during the 8th Plan period is 20,730 MW only, whereas a capacity addition of over 30,000 MW was envisaged. At the same time, the oil consumption in 1994-95 has already touched 60 mt, against indigenous production of around 30 mt, and is projected to increase to 161 mt by the year 2009-10. Correspondingly, the dependence on fossil sources of energy will increase to about 75 per cent of the overall energy demand.

Whereas such a shift towards higher fossil energy consumption and lack of finance pose a major challenge, it also opens avenues to focus efforts on improvement in efficiency of production and use of energy, thereby resulting in saving of energy. Rationalisation in production and use of energy will result in lower energy elasticities and higher GDP per unit energy input.

Energy Conservation and Efficiency Improvement—The Obvious Route

Energy conservation is the only route that can get better mileage out of the available resources. The need is to consider the possibility of evolving an appropriate strategy for energy conservation measures in the country. It is, no doubt, relevant to study the approaches followed in different countries, but it is equally important to understand the impacts felt so far in economic terms because of the conservation measures adopted elsewhere. That will put our approach in the right perspective.

There are also general and obvious points that can get overlooked:

(i) Energy intensity generally falls because productivity gains have raised the value added per unit of energy used, and because of structural shifts in the economy. These changes may have little or nothing directly to do with deliberate efforts to raise energy efficiency.

(ii) Similarly, technological innovations may well have as a by-product the reduction of energy usage, without this having been a deliberate objective. Hence the "natural" turnover of capital stock usually leads to a reduction of energy usage. In the future, this situation may change and accelerate due to shifts in energy policy and prices. In the past there has been little experience of the impact of measures to raise energy efficiency.

It is fortunate that innovations and, above all, turnover of capital stock across the broad economic spectrum result in declining energy intensity. An International Energy Agency Report - "Energy Efficiency and the Environment", 1991, (p. 48) warned: "The progress of energy efficiency with the demand trends examined, needs to be evaluated with care because it is intertwined with so many other factors affecting demand. An energy efficiency improvement is defined as any action by a producer or consumer of energy that reduces the use of energy without affecting the level of service provided".

It is relevant to consider initially the various barriers in terms of institutional, financial and technical arrangements as narrated below:

Barriers to Energy Conservation Efforts

World Energy Council has categorised the barriers as institutional (information), financial and technical. These are listed below:

Institutional

(i) poor information about, and lack of experience, in the energy sector;

(ii) ignorance of what is available in terms of technology and know-how to promote efficiency and proper maintenance;

(iii) bias in favour of encouraging energy provision and usages without similar bias towards efficiency;

(iv) unwillingness to press for full-cost pricing, in developing countries usually for understandable social and political reasons;

(v) opposition from politicians and public revenue officials to the imposition of earmarked taxes to promote energy efficiency;

(vi) poor linkages between utilities and users, and between purchasers and users;

(vii) intellectual property rights, which are intended to reflect the efforts and costs put into developing new ideas, products and processes;

(viii) unwillingness to promote public information compaigns and expose inefficiencies;

(ix) ineffective regulation and labelling;

(x) electoral concerns.

Financial & Economic

(i) perceptions that costs outweigh benefits (despite the fact that payback periods are often in months rather than years, and that some efficiency improvements) can be achieved at close to "zero cost" — even sometimes with net savings;

(ii) difficulty in identifying and calculating savings with precision;

(iii) value of, and returns on, existing assets;

(iv) financial accounting and budgeting methods;

(v) low energy prices, subsidies, and regimes which encourage marginal demand at minimal cost;

(vi) threshold level of energy and cost savings (below which investments do not seem worth making);

(vii) perceived high capital cost of energy efficient technologies as a barrier for poor, heavily indebted countries.

Technical

(i) non-availability of more advanced technology;
(ii) non-availability of new materials and other substitutes;
(iii) infrastructure limitations;
(iv) cultural norms;
(v) tendency toward over-sizing/low capacity utilization;
(vi) lack of research, development and demonstration;
(vii) lack of technical and managerial expertise;
(viii) poor maintenance and lack of spare parts.

Identified Potential Areas for Energy Conservation

The following areas have been identified where specific energy conservation measures can have favourable results: These are mentioned below:

Industrial Sector

Following specific industrial sub-sectors have the largest scope for energy conservation and efficiency improvement without involving heavy modernisation costs:

(i) Processing industries;
(ii) Petroleum refining;
(iii) Aluminium;
(iv) Paper;
(v) Cement;
(vi) Steel;
(vii) Sugar; and
(viii) Copper.

Transport Sector

This will include automobile manufacturing industry as well as road vehicle and railway coach maintenance with emphasis on two wheelers in road vehicles.

Agriculture Sector

Emphasis is to be placed on diesel engines and pump sets and their accessories.

Domestic Sector

Emphasis is to be placed on good housekeeping.

Power Generation and Distribution Sector

Power generation and distribution sector has been identified as a major loss incurring sector. Different steps can be taken which will have a combination of managerial input and technological inputs to bring in higher economic returns.

Sectorwise Issues Supporting Conservation

Industrial Sector

The energy consumption pattern observed in industry during last three years has shown a lowering in energy intensity per unit of industrial production. This is a very positive sign for India where investments in stocks are heavy and foreign investment and private investments are not coming forth. If a lead is to be taken from the recent observations then one has to really appreciate the efforts initiated about ten years back. It is time to intensify efforts to penetrate medium scale and small scale sectors of the industry. It has to be noted that whereas large industries depend for modernisation mostly on the imported equipment, and thereby, they have better access to the latest energy efficient technologies from the international market; the medium and small scale industries largely depend for their equipment and plant on the local manufacturers. In such a case, unless the manufacturers of the equipments and machines are given certain incentives for production of energy efficient machines they may not be motivated to produce energy efficient equipment and machinery; and correspondingly the energy efficiency results may not be very encouraging from the medium and small scale sectors of the industry. It will be necessary, therefore, to think in terms of creating an awareness amongst the users on the one hand and the purchasers of the power driven equipment and machinery on the other. Both will need incentives which shall not be at cross purposes and need not be given in the form of subsidies but basically in the form of tax credits so that they are not constrained by the limited amounts. It should also be remembered that the medium and small scale industries account for 60 per cent of India's exports and any improvement in this sector can significantly contribute in making India's exports far more cost effective.

As far as major industries are concerned, it is necessary to launch immediate campaign in selected industries that are 'large energy consuming' and have the potential to improve through managerial improvements and change in their capital stocks. But this will have a medium term as well as long term perspective.

Transport Sector

As regards transport sector, government's effective Mass Transport Policy will lower energy consumption per capita. But, beyond that, what can be done in immediate term is to convince the individual owners of the vehicles or the transporters on the energy conservation need both from the environmental point of view as well as for making their systems more cost effective. This sector has a very peculiar situation and efforts need to be made on the following two fronts simultaneously:

(i) The manufacturers of the automobiles and transporters must be encouraged through financial incentives and legislative measures to produce energy efficient vehicles.
(ii) The automobile component manufacturers must be encouraged to develop retrofits that will improve the energy efficiency of the existing vehicles.

Certain experiments in the past have shown that energy efficiency upto 30 per cent is achieved if these steps are taken simultaneously.

All this can be achieved through awareness creation.

Agriculture Sector

As regards the agriculture sector, efforts would have to be more or less on the lines of the efforts made in the transport sector. Further, it is also necessary to think in terms of operation and maintenance schedules and patterns of maintenance. It has been observed that upto 30 per cent of the fuel consumed can easily be saved if appropriate steps are taken in this sector.

In the agriculture sector better energy conservation is possible through education of the farmers by the dealers of irrigation pump sets. They need to be educated on the higher energy consumption by an inefficient and ill-maintained pump set or equipment vis-a-vis the optimum possible from a similar efficient agricultural equipment.

In addition, rational fuel/electricity pricing policy shall be another aspect that needs to be properly attended. Although, in the agriculture sector, during the peak seasons, it has been observed that the price of diesel, and even kerosene for that matter, is almost double than the administered price, but the user takes it without any murmur. The subsidised price of electricity, diesel oil and other fuels has resulted in unnecessary waste of energy through inefficient equipment and machinery. Appropriate pricing shall be a major contributory factor in controlling consumption.

Power Generation, Transmission and Distribution Sector

Power generation, transmission and distribution losses must be tackled seriously. The government has already identified this sector for private investment, but so far foreign investments are catering to the power generation side only. The investors are not willing to take any risk with regard to collection of money and creating an infrastructure for servicing.

However, for improving efficiency of the power generating system it will be necessary that while selecting the technology for operation the government goes in for the latest technology whether it is thermal power plants, gas based power plants or hydro power plants.

It is also necessary to focus our attention on the production of different sources of commercial energy like coal and oil. This attention has to be paid over the whole life cycle, including exploration, mining, extraction, washing, transportation, refining and ultimate use as a major source and its by-products. A closer study of upstream and downstream production processes and the end use practices will really develop a strategy for overall energy efficiency improvement in this sector.

Future Conservation Strategy

A strategy for energy conservation and efficiency improvement shall have to be developed.

The *Approach* of the Action Plan for effective energy conservation measure in the country requires following two elements:

(i) *Fiscal Incentives* — the government shall have to provide fiscal incentives linked to energy savings and tax concessions, rather than subsidies;

(ii) *Legislative Measures* — the government shall have to develop an Energy Conservation Act to enforce punitive action under the law and ensure strict implementation.

A four-pronged strategy needs to be adopted with specific time bound programme. The approach has to be pragmatic. Shorter time period, result-oriented programme should call for lower level of technology interventions and lower financial investments. The four-pronged conservation approach shall be as follows:

(i) Better house keeping which may lead to 5 to 10 per cent of energy saving, on an average, in all the four sectors of use. Such an approach can be followed by inculcating the habit of maintaining systems as per the laid down norms. This shall be a low or no investment approach, but shall be universally applicable/acceptable and affordable in every sector.

(ii) Increased efficiency of existing systems mainly retrofitting the production units/equipment with more efficient energy use sub-systems which may result in saving, on an average, of 10 per cent and over at a moderate investment level.
(iii) New technologies that call for introduction of state-of-the-art machines, new processes, etc. which may help in energy saving of 25 per cent and over, on an average. Such an option is highly cost intensive.
(iv) New sources of energy, mainly renewable in nature, may enable a saving of 50-80 per cent. This intervention shall call for change in use pattern and attitudinal change in the user.

A Time Frame shall have to be Developed

The short-term measures would be in terms of improvements in operational measures and the long-term measures would be in terms of strategic improvements and call for large investments. Thus, the following 3-tier time bound Action Plan is suggested:

Short Term Measures	:	1995-1997 (End of VIII Five Year Plan)
Medium Term Measures	:	Upto 2002 (End of IX Five Year Plan)
Long Term Measures	:	By 2007 and Beyond (End of X Five Year Plan)

(i) *Short Term Measures*

These measures will require intensive efforts to promote the following:

(i) Better housekeeping; and
(ii) Increased efficiency of existing systems.

During this short-term phase, initiatives may also be launched to study the options of new technologies and new energy sources.

(ii) *Medium Term Measures*

These will include continuation of activities launched in the short-term, on which government spending will gradually decrease; and to promote introduction of new technologies in terms of state-of-the-art machines and new processes which, in other words, will be justified because of global industrial competition.

Whereas investments in this phase by the government would decrease, the institutional finance requirement would increase.

The target of energy conservation for the 8th Five Year Plan, set by the Government, for 5-year period of 1992-97 has been adopted for 1997-2002, to be achieved in 2002 under medium term of the Action Plan.

(iii) *Long Term Measures*

These need futuristic biological and bio-technological applications and require R&D support.

Conclusion

An effort has been made to outline an approach for energy conservation in the country. However such an effort would require development of appropriate administrative structures and funding.

ANNEXURE-I

GOVERNMENT INITIATIVES SINCE 1973

1974	Fuel Policy Committee Report
1974	Indian Oil Corporation—National Productivity Council-Directorate General of Technical Development. Fuel Oil Conservation Studies in 300 industries.
1976	Petroleum conservation efforts institutionalised by setting up Petroleum Conservation Action Group, later known as Petroleum Conservation Research Association.
1979	Working Group on Energy Policy.
1981	Constitution of Inter Ministerial Working Group (IMWG) on Utilisation and Conservation of Energy.
1982	Setting up of the Department of Non-Conventional Energy Sources (DNES).
1983-88	Setting up of the Advisory Board on Energy (ABE).
1984	Department of Power Identified as Nodal Agency for Energy Conservation.
1987-89	Setting up of the Adviser (Energy Conservation) Office.
1989	Establishment of the Energy Management Centre.

ANNEXURE -II

FISCAL MEASURES

1982	PCRA Boiler Modernisation Scheme.
1983	100 per cent depreciation for notified energy conservation equipment.
1985	Customs duty reduction for fuel efficient vehicles.
1988	Customs duty reduced for notified energy conservation equipment device.
1988	Energy audit subsidy scheme, energy conservation equipment finance scheme.

TWO

ENERGY CONSERVATION IN INDIA: Need and Role of Top Management Commitment

BHASKAR NATARAJAN

Future Energy Scenario

The future of the energy scenario in the country will be characterised by atleast a continuance of the present level of shortages in the near to medium term and a rapid increase in price of energy. The third factor that is likely to be almost forced upon most developing countries is the need for the adoption of high cost technologies for energy production that are likely to minimise the impact of emissions on the environment. The Indian economy has also gone through the first phase of opening up wherein several administrative controls have been removed and there are likely to be more substantial changes in the next phase in the fiscal and administrative control regimes to open up the industry further. The Indian industry is also aggressively exploring foreign markets with a view to increasing exports and this calls for the Indian industry to be extremely competitive.

The reaction of the industry to shortages in the availability of energy has been to install captive diesel generating sets in order to ensure that production levels are not affected. Hence, over the last decade, most industries have installed captive diesel generating capacities almost equal to or greater than their contracted demand with the state electricity boards. Thus, in the absence of power not being made available from the grid, the industry could still maintain their production, although at a much higher cost. In industries where the share of energy cost to the total cost of manufacturing is relatively small (less than 15%), the industries have generally been able to pass on this increase in cost to the customers. This has been possible mainly because the Indian market is in its growth phase and saturation levels and per capita levels of various key consumption items are extremely low. However, in the energy intensive industries where energy costs accounts for anywhere between 20-30 per cent of the total cost of production, these industries have been forced to consider using energy more efficiently with a view to maintaining their competitiveness in the Indian and global markets. Industries in this category mainly include iron and steel, cement, aluminium, paper, fertilizer and textiles, which account for about 60 per cent of the total electricity consumed. Energy conservation and use of energy efficiently is thus one of the more cost effective options to adjust to the energy shortage situation.

Energy Conservation and Efficiency

In the energy intensive industries, major gains have been realised primarily through rapid technological changes. Examples of this are the dry process as against the wet process in the cement industry, the electric arc furnaces versus the conventional method of steel production in the iron and steel industry, and the membrane cell process in the chloralkali industry. However, similar development and efficiency gains have not taken place in the area of utilities such as motors and drive systems and several other commonly used processes in the general engineering industries and other similar categories. The same is the case with electrical appliances that have indeed grown very rapidly during the last decade (10-15%), with no comparable gains in energy efficiency.

The major initiatives from the government in energy efficiency came by way of the Inter-Ministerial Working Group on Energy Conservation that submitted its report in 1983. A separate cell for energy conservation was created in the Ministry of Power (MOP) to coordinate all activities in the area of energy conservation and efficiency in the country. In 1989, the Energy Management Centre (EMC) was set up to provide increased thrust and assume a greater co-ordination role in this vital area. The MOP and EMC have identified several key activities to build capability in the country on energy auditing and management services. Activities have been undertaken with funds from the Ministry's own budget for energy conservation as well as in collaboration with several bilateral and multi-lateral institutions from different parts of the world. The attempt is to identify most energy efficient technologies available elsewhere and to determine to what extent it can be adapted for the Indian conditions.

Discussions with the industry reveal that while there is a reasonable amount of technical information and awareness of energy efficiency and conservation, there is a gap in the commitment that top management gives to energy efficiency. While a large number of industrial units have been carrying out energy audits and are reported to implement the housekeeping and low cost measures for improving energy conservation, the industries have not committed large funds to carry out major energy efficiency investments. The reasons that have been mentioned include disruption to production, maintain market shares even at higher costs, high cost of funds, and doubts about the reliability of new energy efficient equipment and technologies. This paper addresses the need for total commitment from the top management of the industrial units with a view to implementing energy efficiency projects that are comparable to their existing expansion plans or market development activities.

Top Management Commitment

The Top Management Commitment Programme (TMCP) in the United Kingdom has indicated that a specific programme aimed at getting the Chief Executives of major industrial enterprises to commit to energy efficiency does pay rich dividends. Several studies carried out by the Energy Efficiency Office (EEO) in the UK have shown that energy efficiency gains in industrial units that have signed up for TMCP have benefitted substantially, as against firms that had not signed on for such a programme. The important point to note is that this programme is entirely voluntary and there is no legislative or any other statutory backing that forces the industry to join this programme.

The industries, when they sign on, are expected to display their commitment to energy conservation with a declaration signed by their Chairman or Chief Executive Officer and this commitment is displayed publicly at several locations in the industrial unit. The industry also agrees to undertake certain initiatives such as carrying out an energy audit, fixing energy efficient targets and involvement of the entire work force of the industrial unit to energy efficiency. In return for the signed commitment, the industry receives special advice from the EEO on several aspects relating to energy conservation and efficiency. The industrial unit also receives assistance by way of information on financing schemes for energy efficiency and some amount of grant support towards efficiency projects that are likely to attempt some innovative technologies for the first time. As of December 1994, it is reported that about 1800 industrial units have signed on for TMCP. The industrial units which have signed includes several large names such as IBM, Shell, British Telecom, British Gas, GE-Alsthom, Ford (UK), etc. Other countries like Ireland, Denmark, etc have different versions of such a programme.

In India, there is no parallel to the above programme. While several industrial units are carrying out energy efficiency activities in their own limited sphere, there has been no coordinated and concerted effort to ensure that some of the good experiences that some industries have had, are passed on to the others. Also, it may indeed be worthwhile to put together a similar programme that would bring together industrial units to a common platform for initiating activities on energy efficiency. Such an activity normally and naturally be initiated by any of the progressional or sectoral nodal industry associations. Alternatively, initiative can also be undertaken by other institutions such as the Institution of Engineers, Institution of Electrical and Electronic Equipment Manufacturers Association (IEEMA) and other bodies which have the objective of bringing together the industries to a common platform for discussing several other initiatives. The Energy Management Centre could take the lead in putting together such a Commitment Programme implemented by one of the above institutions with whom an appropriate MOU could be signed.

The commitment and participation could be at different levels. The first level would require the industry to sign on and agree to declare their commitment at all their office and manufacturing facilities, form an energy conservation or efficiency executive committee and agree to carry out a detailed energy audit, if one has not been carried out during the last three years, within one year of signing on. The second level commitment could include, in principle, agreement to implement efficiency programme up to a certain level of investments (say upto Rs. 25 lakhs), within say, two years of signing on. The third level commitment could include major retrofitting of equipment, where feasible, and could include specifying industry unit level targets (say up to 10% savings over a two-year period, in energy terms) and thus call for very high level of investments on energy efficiency. Additional details of these three levels are given in Annexure -I.

Targets for Commitment

On the subject of targets for such a programme, it should be possible to design the programme by March 1996 and formally launch the programme in the financial year 1996-97. Aggressive marketing by the EMC and the implementing organizations with key assistance from key chief executives who have a known record of energy efficiency, it should be possible for a target of atleast 50 industrial units to sign on by the end of the Eighth Five Year Plan. Out of these 50 industrial units, while it is expected that almost every unit will sign on for level-I commitment, it should be possible to get atleast 25 per cent of these units to sign on for a level-II commitment. In the Ninth Five Year Plan, we could increase the target for top management programme to an additional 100 industrial units every year with atleast 10 per cent of them signing an agreement for a level-III commitment. This would indeed enable fixing targets for industrial energy efficiency and would also provide an indication to the financing institutions about the extent to which funding would be required for energy efficiency.

It is also important to include in this programme large commercial customers such as hospitals, hotels and office complexes, which have substantial air-conditioning and lighting loads. This could also be taken up simultaneously along with the industrial commitment programme. Another parallel activity that should be initiated is for the industry association and the industrial units to identify other supporting requirements for energy conservation and efficiency such as fiscal incentives, investment facilities and other such requirements to make the programme successful.

However, such an initiative has not come forth from these institutions. Whenever a discussion is initiated for such an activity, everyone agrees that it must be done, but the initiative is implicitly expected to come from the government. Some of the other expectations are that such a programme must be fully funded, with no commitment on targets. When the question of some contribution coming from the potential beneficiaries is raised, the programme comes to a full stop?

There is a strong need for a commitment from the industry to energy conservation. While the argument that industries will do something because they have to survive and make profits does have merit. In actual practice, the statistics do not support this view. Disclosures by the industries in the annual reports do not indicate even a 5 per cent gain in energy efficiency over a 2-3 year period. The immediate need is for commitment based on targets and a simultaneous demand for additional support in any form that is required.

Such a programme will automatically identify requirements of technology in specific areas. It would then be possible to work out detailed programmes to ensure that these technologies come into the market place to further the cause of energy efficiency.

ANNEXURE I

Top Management Commitment to Energy Efficiency and Conservation

The important role of commitment of the top management to energy efficiency and conservation needs no emphasis. The target for the commitment programme should be

(a) Cost reduction of atleast 10-15 per cent within the first two years.

(b) Energy savings of atleast 10 per cent at the unit level within the first-three years.

This commitment can be at several levels.

Level I

Put energy consumption and energy savings as an agenda item for discussion at the next Board Meeting of the company.

Allocate energy consumption monitoring to a member of the top management at the level of Vice-President or Director or Deputy Managing Director.

Energy consumption and monitoring to be discussed atleast once a quarter in the regular ongoing meetings.

Level II

Commitment to carry out a *preliminary energy audit* in the company's premises within the next one year (year 1)

Commitment to carry out a *detailed energy audit* in the company's premises within the next two years, (year 2)

Level III

Implement atleast *50 per cent of the no-cost and low cost measures* identified in the preliminary energy audits within one year of prepaıation of the preliminary audit report (year 2).

Prepare *detailed feasibility reports* for atleast the *top three measures* that would result in maximum cost reduction to the company within one year of preparation of the detailed audit report (year 3).

Level IV

Implement all the measures identified in the preliminary energy audit report (year 3).

Prepare *detailed feasibility reports* for the other measures that have been identified in the detailed audit report that would result in a minimum of 20 per cent cost reduction to the company (year 4).

Implement measures identified in level 3 (year 4).

Commitment to restart at level 1 in year 4

There is a need for continuous feedback of performance and progress review to the Board.

THREE

ENERGY CONSERVATION: Challenges and Opportunities

J.K. DAS

India's per capita primary energy consumption in 1992, inspite of an increase from 113 in 1970 to 226 kilograms of oil equivalent (KGOE), was only about 16 per cent of the world average (1384 KGOE). One of the reasons for such low consumption is that the above figures do not include the traditional energy like fuelwood, animal wastes and agricultural residues which forms a major portion of our total energy consumption particularly in rural areas.

The energy intensities of many developed countries have declined sharply since the first oil shock in 1973. They were able to achieve this by implementing well thought-out policies and programmes of energy conservation. In most of the developing countries, the energy intensities continue to be on higher side. The energy consumption in KGOE per $ of GDP is one of the highest in India at 0.836 against South Korea-0.359, USA-0.343 and Japan-0.132. It gives us a significant scope for energy conservation and calls not only for the continuation and reinforcement of the conservation measures already introduced but also adoption of new and innovative approaches to this issue. Moreover, it is in the context of severely constrained balance of payment position and the grim future prospects that the imperative need for the conservation of petroleum products has to be viewed. Several energy conservation studies conducted by the working groups and experts revealed that our energy use efficiency including oil use efficiency is low as compared to that achieved by the industrially advanced countries. The Inter-Ministerial Working Group has estimated the energy conservation potential to be 20 to 30 per cent in all sectors of the economy.

Challenges Ahead

Considering limited energy resources and utilisation pattern, the following are the major challenges for future:

1. Efficient use and conservation of energy.
2. Reduced dependence on oil and its inter-fuel substitution by gas.
3. Strict demand management of commercial energy.
4. Environment protection.
5. Development of alternate and renewable resources of energy.

All the issues are interrelated needing deliberate and collective efforts to achieve the desired goal.

Oil Conservation Efforts

In India, the focus on energy conservation particularly conservation of petroleum products was initiated with the setting up of the Petroleum Conservation Action Group (PCAG) in 1976; which was later registered as a full-fledged organisation, in 1978, called "Petroleum Conservation Research Association (PCRA)".

The PCRA was entrusted with the following task:

* To create awareness among the people about the importance, methods and benefits of conservation.
* To promote research and development efforts aimed at petroleum conservation in various sectors of economy.
* To promote use of fuel efficient technologies.
* To train and provide technical advisory services.
* To encourage inter-fuel substitution.

During the initial phase of activities PCRA observed that the industrial sector is easily amenable for time bound energy conservation measures. Industrial units and especially the large energy consumers must plan for significant reduction in energy consumption levels. Special attention will also need to be paid in respect of the least energy efficient units. Energy audit and accounting can show the way. Better house-keeping, proper maintenance, efficient management of steam, heat and electrical loads are some of the key areas to act upon. Waste heat recovery systems, cogeneration and utilisation of alternative resources of energy are important measures which can enhance energy conservation levels. Technology upgradation, modernisation and introduction of control instrumentation will be necessary to realise the full potential of energy conservation in industry. In certain basic industries, process modifications or adoption of new technologies will also be necessary. These are the areas where industrialists and technologists need to work closely.

Upto 31st March 1994, PCRA had carried out fuel oil diagnostic studies and energy audits in 3041 industries, with total annual fuel oil consumption of about 5 million kls, and identified a saving potential of 6.11 lakh kls per annum (about 12.3%). Out of this saving potential, industries have been able to realise a saving of about 5.33 lakh kls per annum (10.7% of total consumption) on recurring basis through implementation of the PCRA recommended measures.

PCRA through the above studies, refer Table 3.1, has shown

TABLE 3.1: **Details of Studies Conducted by PCRA**

Type of Industry	No. of Units Surveyed	Annual Consump in lac kl	Saving Potential Identified in lac kl	Saving Potential % of Ann consump	Saving Achvd in lac kl	Saving Achvd % of Annual Consump
Engg.	1136	13.03	1.73	13.28	1.48	11.36
Process	1102	15.79	2.01	12.73	1.71	10.83
Textile	271	5.51	0.61	11.07	0.55	9.98
Glass	144	3.84	0.35	9.11	0.31	8.07
Miscel.	388	11.64	1.41	12.11	1.28	11.00
Total	3041	49.81	6.11	12.27	5.33	10.70

that 54 per cent of the total saving potential could be realised with no or marginal investment by adopting better housekeeping and operational practices. The remaining 46 per cent of the saving potential needs marginal to substantial capital investment. A summary of conservation measures identified by PCRA during its studies as well as estimated percentage saving potential is given below in Table 3.2.

TABLE 3.2: **Conservation Measures and Energy Saving Potential**

Conservation Measure	% Saving Potential	
- Storage, handling & preparation of fuel	5.5	54
- Draft control in boilers and furnaces	25.8	
- Insulation	8.4	
- Condensate/Flash steam recovery/ Plugging of steam leaks etc.	14.3	
- Waste heat recovery	19.0	46
- Other measures (boiler replacement, process modification etc.)	27.0	
	100.0	

To promote oil conservation, PCRA has successfully launched the following major schemes and programmes.

Industries

* Energy Audit Subsidy— 50 per cent of the cost limited to a maximum of Rs. 50,000 per audit.
* Soft loans for boiler modernisation @ 8 per cent interest are extended for the replacement of inefficient oil fired boilers by efficient oil/coal fired boilers—More than 360 inefficient boilers have been replaced with efficient ones under this scheme.

* Development and commercialisation of low excess air film burner—Over 4000 such burners are in use by different industrial units resulting in 10-15 per cent fuel saving.
* Setting up of statewise action groups involving government authorities, oil companies, industries etc to evolve and implement action plans for conservation.

Transport

* Soft loans for replacement of inefficient engines with fuel efficient engines in STUs.
* Setting up of model depots and garages to upgrade operational and maintenance facilities at STUs to demonstrate the benefits.
* Evaluation of additives and devices for fuel economy.
* Setting up of statewise action groups involving government authorities, oil companies, large fleet operators, STUs, etc to evolve and implement action plans for conservation.

All the above efforts have led to improvement in the average KMPL of STUs from 4.01 to 4.41 within a span of 10 years.

Agriculture

* Subsidy for rectification of diesel irrigation pumping systems—More than 5200 such inefficient pumps have been rectified by the PCRA, demonstrating a fuel saving potential of about 30 per cent.
* Subsidy for replacement of in-efficient foot valves in diesel pumpsets

Domestic

* Development and promotion of fuel efficient LPG/kerosene cooking stoves, etc—These fuel efficient stoves are resulting in 20-25 per cent fuel saving compared to ordinary cooking stoves available in the market. About 80 lakh efficient

kerosene wick stoves and 5 lakh LPG stoves are in use in the country.

Research & Development

Realising that any technological breakthrough and its successful commercialisation will have considerable impact on the economy, PCRA promotes and encourages research & development efforts with the help of various R&D establishments, CSIR laboratories, technical institutions, etc for:

— Development of fuel efficient appliances and processes;
— Substitution of petroleum products; and
— Evaluation of additives/devices/appliances for fuel economy.

Emerging Prospects

With the opening up of the Indian economy, the corporate sector for the first time has realised that cost plus pricing will no longer be a sound business strategy. Therefore, a desire to X-ray each element of cost-material, manpower and conversion cost of energy has grown. This is necessary even for survival of various corporate entities. The industry has got to seriously look at bench marking issues like energy cost per unit of output, like any other input cost. The share of fuel costs in total manufacturing cost has gone up by 40-300 per cent depending upon the type of industry. In the competitive environment, owing to increased liberalisation, the industry has to keep vigil on their input costs so as to keep the end-use price more competitive. Accordingly, energy use productivity has to be integrated with other important corporate functions of the organisation.

Promotion of energy conservation in the country would require initiatives in a number of areas like:

— Development of specific oil consumption norms in industries;
— Human resource management—focus on training and

retraining of energy managers;

- Substitution of petroleum products by coal and other products;
- Development of database for evaluation of efficiency standards and improvements required in various sectors/ sub-sectors of Indian economy and their comparison with international standards; and
- Promotion of fuel efficient systems, equipment, appliances, etc.

Module of Education and Training

One more important area requiring such initiative is the development of technical expertise in the country. A conceptual module of education and training on energy conservation as envisaged by IMWG is given below:

Awareness Compaign

Awareness compaign will be aimed at promotional and motivational aspects which can be achieved through assignments, seminars, case studies, publishing of success stories, various reward schemes, etc.

Software Development

Software development includes developing energy data base with respect to

- A system for managing energy conservation programmes in major sectors and indices to be developed and published— It would also highlight sectoral demand, targets and achievements of energy conservation, information on various energy conservation technologies, efficiency parameters/ indices, comparison of Indian technology with that of developed countries for identification of HRD programmes etc.
- Development of specific fuel consumption norms including

bench marking and target setting

- Development of training manuals
- Broad scope of training for engineers and training managers.

Programme for Policy Level Personnel

Appreciation programmes for energy management policies, R&D strategies, monitoring of energy conservation measures, economics of energy use, demand management, technology assessment and upgradation, and International Cooperation.

Programme for Industry Personnel

Tailor-made training packages for energy managers, plant engineers and shop floor operators.

Curricula in Schools/Engineering Institutions

The concept of energy conservation needs to be introduced at the school level as a part of general development of children. Some structured topics concerned with resources and utilisation of energy should be covered in their syllabus with the help of the Ministry of HRD, the National Council of Education Research & Training for school level and the Directorate of Technical Education for Technical Courses.

Further Initiatives Required

To achieve the gigantic task of energy conservation in our country there is a greater need to adopt an integrated approach involving the PCRA, government, industry associations etc in the development, coordination and implementation of energy conservation programmes and activities. Some time bound targets/goals for energy efficiency need to be developed, strategies made and resources deployed to achieve conservation in a concerted manner by one and all concerned with energy.

Initiatives Required at Macro Level

1. There is a need to formulate and implement an integrated energy conservation policy which should lay emphasis on shifting the focus of the country's energy planning process from the supply options to effective demand management. There is a greater need for setting up of agencies for planning, coordination, control and the implementation of energy management and conservation programmes.
2. Institutions and industries concerned with energy should assume responsibility both for generating the awareness in public minds and diffusion of energy conservation programmes.
3. To motivate consumers, methods should be developed and used to influence them to adopt efficient technologies and to reduce barriers. These methods may be in the form of financial assistance and fiscal incentives.
4. Direct contact mechanisms should be developed between the utility consumers, equipment manufacturers and R&D institutes for technological upgradation and efficiency improvement.
5. Changes in the pricing level as well as pricing structure of energy resources may be examined to reflect true economic costs of energy.
6. Energy auditing of all large and medium size industrial units should be made mandatory through the enactment of a suitable legislation.

Initiatives at Micro Level

Industries have a very important role to play in making energy management and conservation programme a success. Some industries have been able to achieve significant savings by adopting conservation measures like waste heat recovery, improved insulation, process modifications etc. In our industries, the following strategies may be worthwhile to pursue:

(a) First, by controlling and optimising energy use in existing plant and machinery through better house-keeping measures, insulation, etc and through retrofitting/replacement of old inefficient equipment with efficient ones, process modification, inter-fuel substitution, etc.

(b) Secondly, by building better energy efficient parameters into the equipment/appliances—The important among these are boilers, furnaces, pumps and motors, internal combustion engines, air conditioning systems, etc.

(c) Energy labelling of equipment, appliances, technologies and processes should be made mandatory.

Conclusion

The high oil intensity coupled with the resource crunch that our country faces calls for a concerted and sustained drive to adopt conservation measures and increase the energy use efficiency. The entire approach to enhancing the efficiency of energy use and bringing down energy consumption levels has to be an integrated one. There is a need to introduce new policy instruments and review institutional framework for lowering energy intensity in general and oil intensity in particular. Over and above its policy and implementation, energy conservation should be adopted as a culture and a habit.

FOUR

ENERGY CONSERVATION : A Perspective

S.K. TEWARI

The worldwide thrust to economic development, especially in developing countries, lays emphasis on sound infrastructural facilities—power being the essential one.

Notwithstanding all efforts, growth in power sector has not been able to keep pace with the demand. Power, being a capital intensive industry, calls for a huge investment—to the tune of 4 crore/MW (approx) of capacity addition. Due to resource crunch, it has not been possible to make investment in power sector on a scale which would match the demand scenario. With actual addition in power generating capacity lagging behind the targeted growth, the wheel of industrialization and mechanization of agriculture is getting retarded causing setback to the process of economic development.

Improvement in Power Utility Operations

While the need for capacity addition is undisputed, the emphasis should also be made on effective utilization of installed capacity (to reap the benefits of investments already made) through economic revival of older units by efficient operation within the specified operation regime and developing strong transmission and distribution network. Although the utilities lay emphasis on power generation programme but they are yet to make a substantial progress in respect of energy conservation. In the changing scenario a well planned energy conservation programme aimed at creating an energy efficient customer by extending utilities, expertise and service need to be evolved. Utilities should extend their expertise and service to customers and create the customer awareness in the efficient usage of energy. This shall go a long way in release of utility's generation capacity for additional uses elsewhere.

In addition to initiative by power utilities, a lead is to be taken by the major industrial players (consumer) who have succeeded in reducing their energy consumption per unit of production comparable with the best at national level or international level. They should impart and share the expertise with the medium and small scale industries, who have less potential for technology upgradation. In fact the big industrial houses should come forward to adopt 4 to 5 medium and small scale industries of their area for such programme implementation.

Data Base on Energy Consumption

In order to implement the energy conservation programme effectively it is imperative to have a realistic data of the present consumption level per unit of production of each industry. It is therefore suggested that the concept of energy auditing should be made mandatory through legislation. National Apex Body for Energy Conservation should extend their help for furnishing the data industrywise to all those industries in the country giving lowest per unit consumption of production both at national and international level. It necessitates a mandatory compliance on the part of concerned industries to observe these requirements both in short, medium and long term perspectives with the final objective to bring down their energy consumption level comparable with the best international standards. As we already know that medium and small scale industries account for 60 per cent of India's export and any improvement in this sector can significantly contribute in making India's exports far more cost effective, the medium and small scale industries should comply with such energy consumption norms set for individual industry and attractive tax benefits and export subsidy should be allowed to these industries to motivate them.

Focus on Agriculture Sector

Another vital sector, namely agriculture sector, has the potential of energy saving to the extent of 30 per cent. The existing subsidised price of energy of the agricultural sector is one of the main reasons in creating an unconcerned attitude in the minds of the farmers for not coming forward to implement the energy saving programme. The first step towards implementing the energy saving programme for agricultural sector is to price the energy appropriately so as to make the user feel the pinch of wasteful expenditure. There needs to be a strong political will to implement this decision. Further, in order to motivate the farmers to purchase the energy efficient implements, the Apex Body should consider giving subsidy to the manufacturers of energy efficient equipments so that cost of technology upgradation is not passed on to the farmers.

The success of the national energy conservation programme will largely depend on creating awareness amongst the common masses through extensive campaigning through the powerful electronic media.

CONSERVATION IN ENERGY PRODUCTION INDUSTRY

FIVE

ENERGY CONSERVATION IN COAL INDUSTRY

R.K. SACHDEV

Introduction

Assured and economical availability of energy is a pre-requisite for economic development of any country including a developing country like India. The share of commercial energy in the total energy use in the country has been progressively increasing in the past decades with around 40 per cent in 1970-71 to around 60 per cent currently. Since no appreciable reduction in the current GDP to energy elasticity ratio of 1.2 is expected in the near future, the commercial energy consumption which is projected to grow at around 6 per cent per annum would go up to 80 per cent of the total energy in the next decade.

Primary Sources of Energy: Relevance of Coal

The primary sources of energy available in India are coal, oil, natural gas, hydro and nuclear power. India's coal resources estimated at 200 billion tonnes, in global perspective, are only about 1 per cent of world coal reserves. India is not very well placed in the sphere of recoverable crude oil reserves and natural gas reserves which are 0.80 billion tonnes and 0.73 billion tonnes respectively. These are likely to last for about 20-25 years at current rate of production. Considering the relatively comfortable resource position of coal vis-a-vis that of hydro-carbon and in view of proven coal reserves in the country of 70 billion tonnes, steady supply of coal at an enhanced level of annual consumption of over 500 million tonnes is likely to be available throughout the next century.

Coal currently meets over 60 per cent of the country's commercial energy supply. The power sector has emerged as the single largest consumer of coal accounting for 67 per cent of total coal consumption and generating over 70 per cent of the electricity in the country. There has been phenomenal growth of the coal based electricity generation capacity which rose from 8000 MW in 1973 to about 51,000 MW at present. The coal based thermal capacity is projected at over 81,000 MW by 2001-02. The electricity sector will, therefore, remain the largest coal consumer in future also.

Given the country's endowment of primary energy resources, it is certain that coal will continue to be the mainstay in providing the increased requirement of commercial energy of the country in the coming decades as well. In view of this, conservation of coal deserves special attention.

Concept of Energy Conservation in Coal Industry

Coal industry has two facets of energy conservation—one as source of energy and the other as consumer of energy.

As provider of the main source of commercial energy of the country, the issue of conservation of coal encompasses the following key areas, namely—exploration; exploitation; beneficiation for improving the quality and efficient utilisation of coal.

As consumer of energy the issue of conservation mainly relates to energy conservation in coal production and energy audit efforts which are similar to those in other industries.

Conservation by Improved Exploration

Conservation of coal resources starts from exploration and proving detailed quality and structure for systematic planning and maximum recovery. For expediting the exploration work and precise delineation of geological parameters, latest technologies like high resolution seismic surveys, inseam seismic surveys, geophysical studies including electrical resistivity, seismic refraction, aerial photography with multispectral scanners etc. are available which need judicious adoption.

Exploitation of coal with maximum possible recovery

More than 60 per cent of the coal reserves are available in relatively thick and steeply inclined coal seams which render the geo-mining conditions difficult resulting in low percentage of recovery through underground mining by currently applied methods. Several steps for conservation through improved recovery percentage are being applied. These are:

- — extension of opencast mining to greater depths;
- — extraction of coal under rivers, railway lines, township etc. by filling the voids with sand;
- — introduction of mechanised longwall mining in congenial geological conditions;
- — Introducing new methods of working thick seams e.g. sub-level caving and gallery blasting;
- — adoption of shield method of mining thick and steep seams of Assam.

While some of the new mining technologies have been introduced with a fair degree of success, in general the results have been mixed. Greater commitment is needed for their successful application on a wider scale.

Beneficiation of Coal for Improving the Quality

Indian coals are generally high in ash content. Further deterioration in quality of coal takes place due to large scale opencast mining. In electricity generating sector poor quality of coal leads to lower availability, higher O&M costs and high pollution at the power plant end; besides higher cost of transportation of coal. Similar problems are faced in other coal consuming sectors due to inferior coal quality.

In the area of coking coal, almost all the coals are being washed before despatch to steel plants. The present ash content of 20-22 per cent in the washed coal against the desired 17±0.5 per cent results in low productivity and higher specific energy consumption. Modernisation of existing washeries has been taken up to further improve the quality of washed coal.

Utilisation of low volatile coking coals is an important aspect of conservation in the coking coal. 20 mt of such coal is being produced currently and are utilised in the industries other than steel. These coals with ash content reduced to 18 per cent by washing have been found suitable for utilisation as blend for steel making. Although action has been initiated to set up a washery for washing such coals, more washeries to wash these coals are required. Concerted efforts are required both on the part of Coal India Ltd as well as SAIL for setting up of more washeries. This will go a long way in augmenting coking coal supplies to steel plants as well as to cut down the imports and to conserve the scarce coking coal.

Non-coking coals are not being washed at present. Some of the benefits arising out of combustion of washed coal at a thermal power station are:

— reduction in emissions;
— reduction in ash handling and disposal costs;
— reduction in oil support;
— higher thermal efficiency;
— reduced load on transportation system;
— increased plant availability;
— increased plant output;
— reduction in operating and maintenance cost.

From these positive aspects of utilisation of washed coal one can safely conclude that this is a right step towards energy conservation through efficient as well as environmentally clean usage of coal. This needs to be brought under the ambit of energy conservation policy for the purpose of fiscal and other incentives.

A beginning in this direction has already been made and two washeries totalling to a capacity of 11 mt are under construction.

More washeries are planned in private sector under B-O-O scheme. Letters of intent, LOI, for four washeries have been issued and action initiated for another three washeries.

Rail transportation being the cheapest and energy efficient transport mode will continue to share about 60 per cent of total coal traffic in the coming years. The following distancewise projections of coal demand would indicate the position that is likely to emerge in respect of transportation of coal to thermal power stations (Table 5.1).

TABLE 5.1: **Distancewise Projection of Coal Demand**

(million tonnes)

Distance	1993-94	1996-97	2001-02	2009-10
Pit-head	61.18	88.10	109.00	127.00
<500 km	38.98	40.90	51.00	58.00
>500 <1000 km	22.48	23.50	30.00	48.00
> 1000 km	42.57	46.50	80.00	175.00
Total	165.21	199.00	270.00	408.00

From the above figures it would be seen that while consumption of mine-mouth power plants will increase from the present level of about 61 million tonnes to 127 million tonnes in 2009-10, power stations located more than 500 km away from the coal sources will consume about 223 million tonnes of coal in 2009-10 against the present level of about 65 million tonnes. This, more than three fold increase, in the consumption in distant power stations will substantially add to the strain on the railway system in the form of high ash in coal besides the problem of handling and disposal of ash at the power plants. In case of other industries located more than 500 km from the coal supply sources, consumption was about 10 million tonnes (excluding steel) in 1993-94, and this is expected to increase to about 55 million tonnes in 2009-10 AD. In this context, beneficiation of high ash coals is particularly relevant.

If all power coals transported over 500 kms are washed, the following orders of savings/benefits can be achieved as shown in Table 5.2.

Direct economic benefits will be available to the power stations

TABLE 5.2: **Savings Through Transportation of Washed Coal**

		2001 - 02	2009 - 10
(i)	Reduction of tonnage to be transported (mt)	15	31
(ii)	Savings in transport cost (Rs. crs)	990	2,273
(iii)	Savings on diesel consumption in transportation (kl)	80,090	1,75,770
(iv)	Reduction in bottom ash (mt)	3	6
(v)	Reduction in fly ash (mt)	10	21
(vi)	Reduction in CO_2 emmisions (mt)	31	65

Note: These numbers are approximate and are based on the presumption that raw coal with >40 per cent ash content will be beneficiated to 34 per cent ash in clean coal.

by way of lower per kwh generation cost and the railways will have an additionality of about 12-14 per cent capacity available at practically no extra investment.

Utilisation of Washery Rejects

The rejects generated on beneficiation of coal contain some burnable coal. In case of three product washing of coal for steel plants, rejects have heat value adequate for utilisation in Fluidised Bed Boilers. Two captive power plants of 2×10 MW capacity each based on washery rejects have been set up and several more sites for such plants have been identified. In case of non-coking coal where heat value of rejects is rather low, some other usage like brick burning will have to be identified for rejects.

Efficient Utilisation of Coal

In view of the limited resource position of coal and its increasing share in the primary energy in India, there is a need for its conservation by efficient combustion. Efforts currently being made by various research institutes, manufacturers of equipment and consumers of coal to promote efficient utilisation of coal need to be stepped up with major sectors like power, steel and cement in particular focus.

Power Sector

The entire capacity in the utility sector comprises of pulverised coal (PC) fired plants. The thermal efficiency of PC fired system is around 32 per cent on an average with little potential for further improvement. It is, therefore, necessary to switch over to the more efficient as well as environmentally friendly coal combustion technologies such as (i) Integrated Gasification Combined Cycle (IGCC); (ii) Pressurised Fluidised Bed Combustion (PFBC); and (iii) Coal Beneficiation and Slurry Combustion (CBSC). These technologies have already been commercially established in some of the advanced countries. We are still planning all the future thermal power stations on the conventional technology. Based on the research work already carried out and the expertise available in the global market, steps should be initiated to set up power plants based on these technologies.

Steel Seetor

Iron and steel industry requires coking coal for the production of hard coke for blast furnace operation. In view of the limited reserves of prime coking coal steps are required for conservation of coking coal through adoption of newer technologies in the areas of coal carbonisation as well as blast furnace operation. Various technologies are, stamp charging, partial briquetting of coal charges and coal dust injection etc. These technologies mostly requires use of non-coking coal thus replacing the scarce coking coal. TISCO have already introduced stamp charging and coal dust injection in its plant. SAIL is evaluating different CDI systems for installing the same in one of its plant.

Energy Conservation in Coal Production

Organised efforts in 'Energy Conservation' in the coal sector were started in early 1987 as a part of the coordinated approach in this direction initiated by the government appointment of nodal officers in the companies, drawing up of short term and long term plans for energy conservation, training of personnel and carrying out "Energy

Audits" were some of the steps taken to implement energy conservation measures in the coal sector. The coal companies since then have reported significant savings in consumption of electricity and diesel in coal mines.

Areas Identified for Energy Conservation/Efficient Use of Energy

Assured power supply particularly in the underground mines of eastern region to ward off excessive energy consumption on account of:

(a) excessive pumping operation due to flooding of dipside working;
(b) low frequency and poor power factor;
(c) standby diesel generation required to maintain hoisting and ventilation facilities required from safety point of view;
(d) ground dumping of coal and its rehandling leading to quality deterioration;
(e) disruption of washery operations requiring restarting and additional consumption of power and deterioration of quality of clean coal.

Notwithstanding these problems, the following areas have been identified for energy conservation/efficient use of energy:

(a) staggering of loads to optimise the maximum demand;
(b) staggering of shifts and off-days;
(c) improvement in the power factor;
(d) setting up of captive power stations for continuous supply of power to deep underground mines and coking coal washeries;
(e) setting up of coal handling plants to size and screen all the coal before despatch.

Improvement in shift utilisation time and equipment utilisation will lead to more efficient use of energy, additionally of coal production and a lower overall specific energy consumption.

With the increasing depth of working and increased mechanisation the specific energy consumption will increase. But with the enforcement of various steps to improve the utilisation of equipment the overall consumption of energy per tonne of production is expected to come down.

Another major area where improvement has to be brought about is through better equipment design. Savings in diesel consumption in opencast mines can be achieved through energy efficient equipment.

Dealing with Coalfield Fires

About 17 sq km area in Jharia coalfield (near Dhanbad) has been affected by fires, some of which started about 70-80 years ago. These fires are reported to have already damaged 37 mt of scarce coking coal reserves and another about 1853 mt cannot be extracted until these fires are fully extinguished. As a result of concerted efforts made since 1971, six fires have been extinguished and spread of another five has been contained. Presently a diagnostic study under a World Bank assisted technical project is in progress. This study is expected to be completed by mid 1996 and aims at development of a comprehensive strategy to deal with these fires. This is a major project aiming at "coal conservation".

Coal Bed Methane

Coal Bed Methane gas (CBM gas), a new non-conventional energy source promises a huge potential for meeting India's energy deficit. This resource, virtually unknown until recent times, has developed into one of the fastest growing energy sector in the United States. In Poland and Russia also similar investigations for assessing the potential of CBM are under way. In Australia, China and elsewhere such investigations are catching up. On a broad estimate, the CBM resources in India are of the order of over a trillion cum mainly in the lower Gondwana coal basins. It is claimed that the mineability of coal does not get hindered by extracting CBM gas. This is another area for undertaking developmental investigation. A number of Indian and foreign companies have evinced interest in development of CBM projects in India.

Molten Carbonate Cell

Another latest technology which has a potential of producing electricity from coal with efficiency level upto 60 per cent is the "Molten Carbonate Cell". Research in the development of Molten Carbonate Cell is in quite advanced stage in Japan and United States. The results available at present indicate that in 7 to 10 years there are going to be major developments in the design of coal based power plants. Since in India we will continue to depend on coal as major source of electricity for many years to come, it is important that we initiate action in undertaking R&D work on this new technology. Ministry of Coal has already decided to take initiative and support an R&D programme on this new development. However, if one or two more user agencies like NTPC, BHEL etc join this effort, we can expect a breakthrough in this field.

Conclusion

Energy conservation in coal industry has two important action components. One dealing with conservation of electricity and diesel oil and steps involved are similar to those followed in any other industry. Second, *inter alia*. deals with conservation of coal resources through application of appropriate technologies for increasing the recovery factor, improving coal quality, dealing with coalfield fires and improved combustion and end utilisation with a view to recovering maximum heat energy out of coal. R&D effort with special focus on efficient combustion technologies like Fluidised Bed Combustion and Integrated Gasification Combined Cycle and Fuel Cell will have to be pursued vigorously. Coal Bed Methane, which is a recent development, holds a great promise in providing a clean fuel to supplement the energy supplies in India.

SIX

ENERGY CONSERVATION IN PETROLEUM INDUSTRY

A. BHATTACHARYAA

Amongst all forms of energy, hydrocarbons continue to be the major source of energy. India being a net importer of hydrocarbons, the management of oil resources is of vital importance to the economic development. Gravity of the situation is evident from the fact that our oil import bill in the fiscal year 1995-96 is about US $ 7.0 billion which is roughly equal to 25% of our total import bill. As the hydrocarbons import consumes a major portion of our foreign exchange earnings (around 32%), it is imperative to minimise the consumption of the same by energy conservation.

Saving in foreign exchange is not the only benefit of energy conservation. Other benefits include increased profits, improved operations, conservation of hydrocarbon resources and reduced environmental pollution. It has been estimated that with effective management of energy and harnessing of ENCON opportunities, saving to the tune of 20% or more in the energy bill are achievable in the petroleum industry. The scope for saving energy could be much higher depending upon the vintage of the technology and the healthy upkeep of the plant and facilities. The present paper deals with energy conservation measures achieved by upstream and downstream public sector oil companies.

Updated in May 1996.

Energy Conservation Efforts at ONGC

The Oil and Natural Gas Corporation (ONGC) and Oil India Limited (OIL), which have been engaged in the exploration, production and transportation of oil and gas, consume significant quantities of energy in different forms. These organisations are conscious of the need for conserving energy and have recognised conservation as an important corporate objective. Their conservation efforts cover prevention of wastage, leakages and losses through various measures. Crude oil and petroleum products, being highly volatile, undergo the process of evaporation and breathing in the course of storage, transportation and handling which result in losses. Leakage, spillage and metering faults also cause some loss. The losses need to be monitored and controlled effectively as loss prevention of even 10-20% can yield substantial savings.

Environment Management

As far back as in 1983 ONGC decided on a statement of Corporate Environment Policy. A lot of importance is attached to environmental and social obligation. ONGC published the first ever Five Year (1985-90) "Environment Management Plan" for environmental safeguards, enabling advance planning in this regard. Now, one of the corporate objectives of ONGC is environment protection. The organisation has set up a full-fledged Department of Safety and Environment Management and has introduced a well conceived system of environmental information and awareness as well as monitoring implementation of standard industrial practices for maintaining a clean and safe environment. ONGC has also established an Institute of Petroleum Safety and Environment Management (IPSEM) to provide R&D support to environmental aspects.

Energy Conservation during Drilling

Energy consumption for various activities like drilling, production, cargo operations, LPG production, etc are monitored, operationwise and regionwise. The consumption patterns of operations are analyzed and the strategies to cut down the consumption rate are evolved from time to time. The fuelwise consumption pattern, for 1995-96, is as follows: natural gas 87.0% [1227 million metric standard cubic metre, MMSCM]; HSD/Petrol 11.0% (201.2 Mltr) and electricity 2.0% (337.5 MU). Emphasis is being laid on maximizing the usage of natural gas thereby reducing the consumption of liquid petroleum products. The liquid petroleum products consumption in ONGC was 18.0% less in 1995-96 (201.2 Million ltr) when compared to base year 1989-90 (245.28 Million ltr). Energy audits are being conducted for identifying and locating energy intensive units and plants. Specific improvement programmes are being designed suiting the needs of particular site/equipment. Various conservation measures have been adopted like use of lube oil analysis kits, conversion of diesel engines into dual fuel (gas + HSD) operation, by using gas engines in place of diesel engines, CNG for automobiles and gas turbine generator sets. Pilot project using CNG in place of diesel/ petrol in various types of vehicles and generators have been conducted successfully in Bombay, Tripura, Gujarat and Southern Region. Various automobiles converted are Ambassador car, jeeps, trucks and buses, which have been successfully trial tested. Natural gas based, 90 ton absorption chilling A/C systems have been installed for centralized air conditioning at Nazira, ERBC. They are substituting the consumption of electrical energy by natural gas.

Waste Heat Recovery Systems

ONGC is using waste heat recovery systems at major installations like offshore platforms for well fluid heating, glycol heating, PPD storage tank heating and other process heat requirement, offshore drilling rigs for generation of potable water through waste heat recovery water makers and cogeneration is used at one shore processing complexes of Hazira and Uran, through waste heat recovery boilers installed in conjunction with two 20 MW gas turbines at each complex. By using various energy efficient measures like waste heat recovery, use of soft-starters, variable frequency controllers, solar energy, efficient lighting fixtures etc, savings to the tune of Rs. 107.67 crores had been achieved during 1995-96.

Measures to Maintain Ecological Balance

Various steps have been taken by ONGC to protect the environment and different pollution control measures have been implemented to maintain ecological balance during land acquisition.

Development of Site

Drilling locations sometimes fall on forest land necessitating felling of trees and bushes, and sometimes displacement of inhabitants. In such cases ONGC acquires equivalent land area somewhere (preferably nearby areas) and hands it over to the forest department for development purpose. During the development stage of a drilling location, attempts are made to plant trees, bushes and grass of compatible and fast growing nature so as to minimise the effect on flora and the fauna. Bunds are made wherever necessary to avoid soil erosion.

Cluster Drilling

Steps have been taken to minimise use of land by drilling a number of wells (usually 3 or 5 wells) as far as possible from a common platform i.e. same location.

Social Programmes

Along with the development of drilling sites ONGC also takes steps and implements social programmes like construction of roads, drains, bridges and socio-economic development of the area.

Measures to Control Environmental Pollution during Drilling

Measures taken by ONGC to control environmental pollution caused by drilling operations are as follows:

— *Ring Bund:* A cement plastered brick walled ring bund of 3-4" height with 1" deep plastered foundation is constructed on the periphery of each drilling site to prevent seepage, leakage or overflow to the adjoining field.

— *Compartmentalisation of drill site:* Drill site is generally compartmentalised into three segments so as to avoid intermixing of drilling fluid containing different chemicals, burnt oil/grease and water (rain/technical water).

— *Cutting Pit:* A cutting pit is made to collect the rock cutting of well separated from drilling fluids at surface, along with washings of solid removal equipments.

— *Waste Pit:* Waste pits are constructed to receive various streams of effluent. Their capacities range from 2000 to 4000 cum in case of cluster drilling and 3000 cum in case of normal drilling. To check seepage/leakage from waste pit, following points are taken care of: (a) Minimum distance from waste pit boundary wall is kept at 1.5-2.0 m; (b) Use of synthetic impervious sheet lining/cement plastering particularly in areas having unconsolidated soil conditions; and (c) Filter system is provided in compartments of the waste pit to contain oil and heavy solid particles.

— *Oil Pit:* All the oily effluents containing mainly burnt oil and grease are collected separately in oil pits constructed for the purpose.

— *Skimming of Oil:* Use of an oil skimmer practiced for manual skimming of oil floating on waste water and transported to GGS for disposal.

— *Control Water Use:* Care is always taken to minimise use of water for operational purpose. Refuse of untreated effluent water from drilling fluids practiced for cleaning purpose of derric floor and solid control equipment (desander, desilter, shale shaker, etc,). Recycling of engine cooling water is saving 2-3 cum water per day.

— *Treatment in Pits:* Effluent water collected in pits is treated with lime and alum in a specified pit to make it fit for operational use through recycling.

— *Modified Filtering Arrangement:* Modified filtering arrangement in pits is also practiced in some drill sites. Here, alum and lime treatment is given to a treatment tank placed in between waste pit and other pits having arrangement of filter compartments. The treatment and filtered water which is very clear is used for operational purpose.

— *Skid Mounted Effluent Treatment Plant:* A skid mounted chemical treatment plant consisting of 3 nos metallic tanks of 30-40 cum capacity with in-built arrangement for chemical treatment (lime and alum) of effluent water for recycling purpose is under process of fabrication for installation at a drill site. The plant has conceived the principles of (a) removal of oil/grease by absorption; (b) sedimentation of solids; and (c) filtration thereon from muddy effluent water from waste pit to obtain clear water for operational purpose. It has the capacity to generate 30-35 cum clear water from waste water in each batch within a time span of 6-7 hours. The plant can be transported from one drill site to another drilling location along with the movement of the rig.

Measures to Control Environmental Pollution during Production

Measures taken by ONGC to control environmental pollution caused by production operations are as follows:

— *Oil Pit:* Oil produced during production testing of an exploratory well is received in a specified cemented oil pit and thereafter it is despatched to group gathering stations, GGS through pipe line/tanker. In case of development well, oil/gas found is directly flown to GGS.

— *Effluent Water:* The effluent /waste water separated from crude oil at GGS is evaporated at evaporation pit through flaring of associated gas.

— *Gas Flaring:* To control the pollution by the associated gas of crude oil, the flaring of the same at GGS is accomplished in a flaring pit near GGS further, flare area is enclosed completely by asbestos/cement sheets in addition to the compound wall followed by multipoint flare of 6-8 points and of low height is ensured over elevated single point flare.

— *Removal of Oil in Winter:* During winter, oil floating on water in oil pit is converted to semi solid state and collected through skimming manually and transported to GGS for disposal.

After completion of drilling operation following steps are taken by ONGC for pollution control.

— Serviceable drilling fluid left over after drilling operation is transported to next drill site to reuse in the coming up well. All oily effluents (mixed with burnt oil, grease, etc) of pits are transported to GGS through tanker for disposal.
— Unwanted material like scrap, wire ropes, debris, solid, etc are cleaned and drill site levelled properly.
— All the pits of drill site are initially filled with rock cutting followed by earthen materials such that level of earth work comes upto normal ground level.
— Leaving the area earmarked for X-mass tree and oil pipe line connected to GGS, all other area of left over drill site is cleaned and levelled properly, and made easily approachable.

After completion of drilling and production operations, approximately 1000 trees are planted at each drill site to beautify the environment and improve ecology. Fast growing trees such as Gulmohar, Accasia, Eucalyptus, Pink Asia, Ashoka, Bamboo, are planted. Trees are also planted on strips of road leading to the well sites and also to GGS. During 1990, 1518 nos of plants were planted in Borholla Changpang field of DVP. Upto the year 1995-96, around 22 lakh trees have been planted.

Environmental Pollution Abatement Measures by Oil India Limited

Potential environment pollution hazards associated with an oil industry includes pollution of air, water and soil. It has always been the philosophy and moral obligation of Oil India Limited (OIL) to focus on the concept of a clean environment which dates back to the early part of the sixties i.e. almost from the year the production has started. The liquid effluent generated from the drilling and workover wells is source of pollution to the nearby terrestrial and aquatic eco-system. In the earlier days, this liquid effluent was being contained in makeshift pits without any scientific design in their construction. However, over the years OIL has developed a scientific way to drilling effluent management by adopting the following processes as of now:

— The effluent pits are scientifically designed having calculated capabilities.
— The pit walls are made impervious by brick soiling/lining etc, wherever required.
— The pits are compartmentalised for more effective mopping of floating oil.
— The concept of central effluent pit/emergency pit has been introduced to cope with situations of heavy rains and prolonged monsoon, which is an inherent problem in the oil fields in the north eastern region.
— Also mobile effluent treatment plants are being tried out for on the spot treatment and discharge of drilling effluent and refuse successfully recently, as also utilising the solid waste generated from drilling activities for land filling.

OIL's future plan in environment management envisages implementing the recycling technology for all drilling wells in various operational areas and reclamation of the land utilised for drilling purpose for bringing back original condition of the same. High oil content (1000-3000 ppm), dissolved solid content (5000 ppm to 8000 ppm) against around 100 ppm in surface stream etc in the formation water negates the possibility of disposing the same in the surface streams.

The formation water was being managed by partial evaporation and disposal in the earlier days of the oil production. For better management of the pollution hazard arising out of produced formation water, OIL is adopting the following processes at present.

— Formation water is disposed in disposal wells specially drilled for the purpose, having impermeable layers.

— The water sample from potable water are regularly monitored to ensure that the discharged formation water does not contaminate the aquifers.

— To overcome the problem of formation clogging due to oil presence in the disposal of untreated formation water, water is treated in the formation water treatment of plants adopting the process of gas/air floatation and filteration thereby reducing oil content to less than 10 ppm and turbidity to almost nil, making it more suitable for disposal.

— The other action taken is to change the earlier practice of using water soluble demulsifiers to oil soluble demulsifiers. By using the oil soluble demulsifiers, water clearing plants and proper flocculates, the oil content in formation water is reduced to below 10 ppm and clear formation water is injected back to the formation, serving the dual purpose of reservoir pressure maintenance and better environmental management.

The factor mostly responsible for air pollution in an oil industry is the flaring of gas. Apart from heat and light that it emanates, the components of concern in the natural gas flares. To reduce the effect of heat and light, while earlier the flare pits were surrounded by only metal sheet drums, they have been replaced by asbestos sheet walls.

Further, the following improvements in the system, have been made.

— The flare pits are provided with brick walls with refractory lining.

— The pits have multiburner facility with downward tilt instead of a single burner.

— To reduce the luminosity of the flame, pits have been designed for abundant supply of air.

— Proper separation at each unit is ensured to avoid liquid carry over while flaring.

— The gas produced from the fields in the north eastern regions is free of sulphur. As such, there is no SO_2 component in the flare. Also the abundant supply of air restricts the formation of CO. Experience over the years has established that there is no harmful effect caused by such flares on the environment due to the above mentioned reasons. To substantiate the above facts in a more scientific way, OIL has procured a mobile air quality monitoring laboratory at a cost of about Rs. 27 lakhs. The ambient air quality of the oilfield area is monitored on a regular basis and the reports are studied.

— The bulk of the gas produced in OIL's fields is the associated gas. OIL uses this gas as fuel for number of internal operations, reservoir pressure maintenance purpose, and supplies to external consumers of downstream industries. Working within various constraints like low upliftment by consumers, lack of infrastructural facilities etc OIL however has been able to bring down the total flaring of gas to approximately 1.20 mmscmd at present (1995-96) from a level of 1.69 mmscmd during 1985-86 by taking some of the steps as enumerated below:

— Improved operation efficiency of existing compressors.

— Procurement of new compressors.

— Improvement in the gas pipeline network etc.

— A sophisticated underground gas storage scheme has successfully been implemented by OIL. The storage scheme has the facility to store surplus associated gas upto 0.8 mmscmd in four of the non-associated gas reservoir with facility for reproduction at the time of need. This not only avoids wastage of gas but also helps in protection of the environment due to low gas flaring. Microprocessor based Supervisory Control and Data Acquisition (SCADA) system recently installed will closely monitor and control the storage and production operations based on market gas offtake fluctuation. With the commissioning of NEEPCO Power Plant at Kathalgur, the gas flaring is expected to be reduced to the minimum.

Role of Petroleum Conservation Research Association

After the first oil shock in 1973-74, the need for finding ways and means of conserving petroleum products was recognized and for this purpose, apart from taking stray measures in different fields on a limited scale, the Ministry of Petroleum and Natural Gas set up an organisation known as Petroleum Conservation Action Group in 1976 which was registered as a society in 1978 under the name of Petroleum Conservation Research Association (PCRA). All the public sector oil companies, the Indian Institute of Petroleum and the National Productivity Council are its members. Its main functions are to initiate, coordinate and promote programmes for the conservation of petroleum products in the industrial, transport, agricultural and household sectors. The thrust areas are, e.g., the creation of mass awareness on the need for the conservation of petroleum products and promotion of measures to conserve such products by curbing wasteful practices and improving the oil use efficiency of equipment, engines and appliances. Its major activities are field surveys; energy audits; diagnostic studies; R&D work; training and education of the consumers in various sectors of the economy.

Energy Conservation Efforts at Indian Oil Corporation

The need to create greater awareness of fuel conservation efforts was accentuated by the Gulf crisis, and the Government of India introduced a number of new measures to reduce consumption of petroleum products. In addition to demand management, Indian Oil Corporation (IOC) organised a number of seminars, workshop and campaigns to propagate fuel conservation to cover all sectors of the economy. IOC has been maintaining the thrust on conservation of fuels at all its units. Revamping of Atmospheric Vacuum Unit (AVU) I and II, Barauni Refinery, which was completed during the year, is expected to result in fuel savings of 13,200 tonnes per annum. Other schemes under various stages of implementation at refinery locations will contribute to fuel savings of 37,890 tonnes per annum on completion. In addition to demand management, the Marketing Division of IOC adopted sixteen states for a concerted conservation action plan. To promote LPG conservation, the Bureau of Indian Standards (BIS) was persuaded to upgrade thermal efficiency of LPG hot plates from a minimum level of 62% to 64%. To popularise use of fuel efficient NUTAN Stoves, a media campaign has been launched. The various conservation efforts by the Division resulted in savings of fuel and lubricants estimated at Rs. 100 crores during the year 1995-96.

Energy Conservation at Refineries

The refineries have been taking a variety of managerial operation and investment related measures for conserving fuel and minimising its loss. While the success achieved by the individual refineries varies, the overall energy consumption plus loss in all the refineries put together has decreased by more than one per cent during the last five years. The annual savings achieved by the refineries through energy conservation projects and measures works out to around 0.25 mt of oil valued at about Rs. 40 crores.

Energy Conservation Efforts during Seventh and Eighth Plans

The steps taken in the Seventh Plan period (1985-90) for energy conservation in the refineries, which are intensified further during the Eighth Plan period (1992-97) include: regular comparison of energy and loss consumption levels in the refineries; internal/external audits of the performance levels; improved housekeeping arrangements; and institution of energy conservation awards for the refineries. Besides, during the Eighth Plan period (1992-97), the efficiency of the oil-fired equipment (furnaces and boilers) was increased through modifications/replacements, recovery of pre-heat from the hot refinery streams has been optimised, and regular energy conservation cells have been set up in each of the refineries for monitoring energy conservation performance and drawing up future plans/projects. With the setting up of a conservation cell in the Ministry of Petroleum & Natural Gas (MOPNG), this aspect is now being monitored more closely.

Plans for the Ninth Five Year Plan

During the Ninth Plan Period (1997-2002), it is proposed to concentrate on such areas as: the application of new technologies/techniques like the PINCH Technology for maximising the recovery of pre-heat from hot streams; use of low level heat, wherever available, for water purification etc.; reduction in the consumption of fuel in power generation; and reduction in the steam consumption levels. The refineries have already implemented projects to achieve a saving of about 2,50,000 tonnes of fuel per annum during the Eighth Plan period, and further work is in hand to identify the projects which would yield additional savings as given below:

Name of the Project	PSU/Company	Total Cost (Rs. Crores)
ENCON projects for increasing efficiency	IOC	112.0
ENCON projects at Bombay & Vizag Refinery like new FCC Feed Furnace/crude preheat optimisation, replacement of low efficiency furnace, flare gas recovery etc.	HPCL	50.0
ENCON project like steam generation facilities for Visbreaker charge heater crude/preheat train optimisation/low level heat recovery etc.	CRL	30.0
ENCON projects	MRL	40.0
ENCON scheme	BRPL	6.3
Heat integration of CDU and Vaccum units	BPCL	14.6
Replacement of old boilers	BPCL	14.0
	Total	266.9 crores

A system of advanced process controls has recently been introduced by the Madras Refineries Limited for optimising the refinery operations, leading to the improved product yields and minimising energy consumption. A plan has been drawn up to install this system during the next couple of years at other refineries where computer control systems are already available. For the remaining refineries, the existing instrumentation systems are proposed to be replaced by electronic/computer controlled systems: and advanced process control systems are proposed to be introduced progressively.

To bring down the consumption of lubricants, action plan has been drawn up by Ministry of Petroleum and Natural Gas (MOPNG) as follows:

(i) MIL-B level oil has a drain interval of about 9000 Km and MIL-C has a drain interval of 18,000 Km. The use of MIL-C can result in saving of atleast 25% at present. The saving can and should be further improved with the use of oil filters of matching performance, the manufacture of which also needs to be promoted.

(ii) The campaign launched by the oil companies at the retail outlets and through the media need to be continued to promote the use of 2T oil in small two-stroke engines.

The quality of petroleum products has a direct bearing on the efficiency of their use although to realise tangible benefits, suitable modifications may be required in the equipment. The product quality improvements, can therefore, facilitate conservation of petroleum products and improvements, can, therefore, facilitate conservation of peroleum products and may also help reduce the environmental pollution level. MOPNG has already planned a phased reduction in the lead content of motor spirit to 0.15 gm per litre maximum by 1993-94 and lowering of the sulphur content of diesel fuel to a maximum of 0.5% by 1996-97. Further, suitable changes in the specifications of kerosene and Naphtha are proposed to be introduced to assess their impact on efficiency.

Thus, oil sector has taken several initiatives for conservation of hydrocarbons. Necessary measures, including: use of inert gas for ocean transport, improved metering and measurement of crude oil and products, better house keeping and close monitoring have been implemented to reduce the loss of crude oil and products in their transportation, storage, handling and distribution.

India, as a signatory to the Rio Convention, is deeply concerned about degradation of human living environment. Our legislation requires that rigorous environmental impact assessment be prepared for all projects including petroleum, during the planning and approval process. More recent guidelines of the Ministry of Environment and Forests cover the conservation of biological natural resources and their eco systems and water pollution control. MOPNG is aware that during the last decade, public concern on the environment has grown tremendously towards energy efficiency, conservation and potential negative environmental impact associated with the development of petroleum resources. Natural gas is recognised as having less pollutants and considered more environment friendly. One of the key areas of focus in the formulation of MOPNG's long range development plans is to ensure that environmental considerations are fully integrated into sustainable development.

ROLE OF INDUSTRY ASSOCIATIONS

SEVEN

ENERGY CONSERVATION MEASURES: Role of Chambers of Commerce

V. RAGHURAMAN

The uncaging of the Indian tiger buttressed by the liberalisation process in progress has presented the Indian business community an opportunity to integrate into the global market. With the possibility of setting up ventures keeping the entire world market in view has opened up new vistas. To be global players, Indian business has to gear itself to be competitive in terms of quality, delivery and price of products and services. This is possible only if sustained and innovative strategies are adopted for enhancing productivity, efficiency and effectiveness of systems.

Energy being the prime mover of industry is critical for industrial growth. For long, power generation and transmission and distribution, oil refining and coal mining and distribution as well as pricing have been state controlled. Only now opportunities are emerging for the entry of private sector. There have been gaps between demand and supply especially in the electricity availability due to a plethora of reasons, the notable being paucity of capital, non-availability of capacity due to managerial and skill deficiencies and ineffective linkages.

The liberalisation policies to succeed call upon industry to chalk out strategies for assessing the energy requirements on a reliable basis and also rationalise its use in order to minimise the energy inputs in productive operations, i.e. minimise specific energy consumption. Details of ASSOCHAM's efforts are given in the Annexure.

High Energy Intensity of Manufacturing Sector

Energy intensity of the Indian manufacturing sector is high in practically all sub-sectors compared to the developed and in some cases developing countries. Over the years, concern has been expressed over this disquieting aspect, and the question of fixing norm of energy consumption for typical sub-sectors such as steel, cement, pulp and paper, etc have been suggested by government agencies, industry associations and academics. Such suggestions are not necessarily followed up to the logical conclusion. Evolving norms require sustained and continuous effort; enthusiasm usually drops when it is realised that norm building exercise is tedious and time consuming. The reason is obvious—there are many variations due to technology choice, economies of scale, specific characteristics of raw materials, product mix, plant age, capacity utilisation, etc.

Within the country itself one perceives wide variations in energy consumption within a sub-sector for example in the steel sector the consumption varies from 8.7 - 15 G cal/tonne of crude steel. The figure for developed countries is 4-6 G Cal/tonne of crude steel. The energy consumption trends in SAIL plants indicate a lower consumption with advancing years:

Year	Energy Consumption G Cal/ tonne Crude Steel
1984	11.2
1987-88	10.2
1989-90	10.2

Hence, it would be worthwhile to consider the international and national norms and compare the norms to a particular unit, allow for variations and set norms based on realistic, achievable parameters. Otherwise blindly fixing norms without ground realities will be counter-productive.

Consumption Pattern

Keeping this in view, and also to understand the state-of-the-art of energy consumption in the industrial units and the energy conservation efforts initiated by them, Chambers of Commerce in India have undertaken surveys from time-to-time. The survey by ASSOCHAM in 1991 covered the sub-sectors of chemicals, cement, engineering and automobiles, polymers and rubber, metals, textiles, leather and food industries. The study revealed that in general large industries were found to be well organised and well informed in energy audit subsidy schemes and equipment financing for energy conservations schemes. Such awareness was not generally evident with medium and small scale industries.

Several of the industrial units have undertaken energy audits with professional assistance from outside consultants. Large organisations like NOCIL, Orissa Cement, SRF, L&T, Union Carbide, etc have their own in-house audit teams. Companies like ACC and Chemplast have energy audits which are undertaken as a regular exercise and results constantly monitored. Quite a few companies like Mukand Ltd have energy cells under the leadership of a Vice-President. Bata India has framed a slogan 'War against Waste'.

The percentage share of energy cost in total cost varied from a low of 0.36 per cent in Capol Farm Equipment Ltd to as high as 65 per cent in Chemplast. Energy costs varied owing to the processes of production, products involved, size of turnover and the sources of energy. An important indicator there was the tremendous potential for conservation in industries which were intensive users of energy, such as chemicals, cement, plastics, metals, etc. Serious and sustained efforts at energy saving by such industries could lead to substantial reduction in their cost of production which, in turn could help them become much more competitive. Engineering industry and automobiles indicated a variance of 0.36 per cent to 3.21 per cent, cement - 21 per cent to 36 per cent, plastics - 6 per cent to 30.96 per cent, textiles - 0.33 per cent to 10.4 per cent and metals - 3.34 per cent to 7.3 per cent. This could be a reflective indicator for many other companies in similar industries for the purpose of comparative analysis.

Consciousness in Industry

Thus, there has been a general level of consciousness among

industrial units in reducing wastage, improving housekeeping, installation of production machinery with improved technology, cogeneration system, etc. Polychem Ltd, for example, installed a medium pressure boiler of better efficiency which led to reduction of fuel oil consumption, resulting in a saving of Rs. 6.0 lacs. Modi Xerox have installed shunt capacitors and photo cells in street lights in their complexes. Similarly, Albright Morarji & Pandit Ltd have installed additional capacitors to improve the power factor.

The survey findings have been published by ASSOCHAM with factual information on the measures implemented by the industrial units in reducing their levels of energy consumption. ASSOCHAM has in collaboration with Doordarshan developed video films for public dissemination. FICCI has also conducted surveys and published their findings which are in line with ASSOCHAM's own findings. CII has been publishing regular newsletters incorporating success stories. Several industry associations have also been following this trend. Most of the associations have also been interacting with Government sponsored organisations like Energy Management Centre, National Productivity Council, Petroleum Conservation Research Association in conducting seminars, energy audits, etc. The PHD Chamber of Commerce and the Maharashtra Chamber have been implementing the Energy bus programmes of the UNDP and the EEC sponsored by the Energy Management Centre. Thus there has been a fair amount of involvement of the Chambers of Commerce in energy conservation efforts in the country.

National Data Bank Necessary

However, a lot remains to be done. Energy audit manuals of specific industry sub-sectors need to be developed and the energy consumption levels of Indian industry properly catalogued for developing industry-wise profiles and comparing their performance over the years. This calls for the setting up of a National Data Bank which can be very well served by a nodal organisation such as the Energy Management Centre, networking with Chambers of Commerce in the country. The Chambers of Commerce can also set up demonstration centres with simulators to training aids as well as pilot plants for imparting training and industrial personnel in carrying out their jobs with better skills and knowledge base.

Conclusion

There is thinking at different levels of government that the Chambers of Commerce are to be involved in managing the energy management systems. This thought needs to be considered carefully and implemented logically in order to make Indian industry energy efficient.

ANNEXURE

ASSOCHAM'S ENERGY CONSERVATION EFFORTS

ASSOCHAM has an Expert Committee on Conventional and Non-Conventional Energy with 58 professionals from its membership and from other specialised bodies serving on it. In the field of energy, it is our endeavour to disseminate maximum information possible for the benefit of the industry and at the same time propagate the concept of energy savings. The Energy Division provides several services like:

- Advisory services to achieve savings in energy.
- Training programmes on energy efficiency and conservation.
- Information dissemination on key issues related to energy.
- Conferences, seminars and workshops on general energy policy issues, roundtable discussions with senior government officials.
- Undertake studies in various aspects of energy use, policy matters of government and industry.
- Undertake specific projects with the objective to enhance energy efficiency and promote private investments in energy sector.
- Interaction with visiting experts from abroad to facilitate mutually beneficial proposals.
- Identification of business/investment opportunities in the field of energy.
- Publications of energy related monographs, technical papers, backgrounder etc.

Energy Publications

Publications of topical interest have been brought out from time to time, viz. Energy Conservation in Indian Industry, Private Sector Participation in Power Generation, Consumption Trends of Petroleum

Products in Select Industries, Non-Conventional Energy Sources and Energy Management, and Energy in India's Economic Development. ASSOCHAM in association with Delhi Doordarshan has produced a five series television programme on the Energy Conservation achievements of the select Indian companies.

ASSOCHAM brings out quarterly publication "Energy Tracks", which carries information on Policy Measures, News Brief, New Technology Developments, Tips on Energy Conservation and other issues related to Energy in India and abroad.

EMCAT Project of USAID through IDBI

ASSOCHAM has undertaken a Project titled "Improvement of Energy Efficiency" in Foundry Industry of Agra, Glass Industry of Firozabad and Pottery Industry of Khurja. The Project covers dissemination of information and creation of awareness on the possibilities of improving energy efficiency ratios. Under the project activities, several workshops, training programmes and discussions were organised. Besides this, poster on energy conservation was made, three video-films both in English and Hindi were produced. Efficiency monitoring was carried out in the three places in association with National Productivity Council with use of their Energy Bus.

ASSOCHAM's Study—Energy Conservation in Indian Industry

ASSOCHAM conducted a detailed survey to assess the Indian Industry's attitude towards energy conservation. The study is titled "Energy Conservation in Indian Industry". The observations made in the survey paint both a bright and a grim picture, thereby indicating that much is desired to be done in the field. Major industrial heads covered were: Chemicals, Engineering and Automobiles, Cement, Plastics and Polymer, Rubber and Leather, Textiles, Metals, Foods, Paper, and Electricity Generation.

It was observed that quite a few organisations were not aware of the major energy conservation schemes being offered by the governments and financial institutions. Larger organisations were, however, more informed about the schemes and many of them had availed of them as well.

Energy Audits to Find Potential Energy Saving Areas

Some of the companies under all industrial heads, have undertaken energy audits. Many of them have resorted to professional assistance to explore potential energy savings areas. Some companies even have their own in-house audit teams. Others undertake energy audits as a regular exercise and also monitor the results thereof. Few others have established energy saving targets vis-a-vis their total costs. The survey indicates that most of the companies are concerned about rising energy costs and are regularly making efforts to control them.

Efforts to Conserve Energy

All the companies have made positive efforts to conserve energy and have taken steps to avoid its wastage. Improved house keeping, installation of production machinery with improved technology, retrofitting, improvement in production process like waste heat recovery and insulation, regular servicing of machines, installation of captive electricity generation plants and use of improved raw materials in production are some of the methods which have been implemented by the companies to reduce energy costs. Educating workers on the importance of conservation is another step that many companies have undertaken. In most cases, the conservation measures have shown positive results. Several companies have undertaken in-house research and have invented original equipment which have led to avoidance of energy wastage, resulting in lower operational costs.

Alternate Sources of Energy

Many respondents have indicated making use of alternative/ nonconventional sources of energy. Some of them have achieved considerable success with their efforts and have plans to expand their usage significantly. Use of solar heater for heating water and furnace oil was found to be the most common. Other sources like wind, biogas, rice husk and lignite, in place of coal, and use of exhaust gases were also mentioned.

Some of the organisations which were covered in the survey have indicated handsome figures in terms of money saved over the years through energy conservation as shown in the following table:

TABLE

	Company Name	Total Savings
1.	NOCIL	126 crores
2.	Herdillia Chemicals Ltd.	170 crores
3.	SRF Ltd.	189.3 lakhs
4.	Saurashtra Cement & Chemicals Ltd.	200.0 lakhs
5.	ACC Ltd.	8 crores
6.	Mukand Ltd.	3 crores
7.	Tube Products India	13 lakhs
8.	Union Carbide Ltd.	66 lakhs

Every year appeals are made by the President of ASSOCHAM for conserving energy. Seminars, workshops, training programmes and round table discussions are regularly organised by ASSOCHAM at various cities.

Several important issues have been raised by ASSOCHAM in various forums which have caught the attention of many. One of the major issues is the formation of an integrated energy policy which would cover all aspects of energy and its overall development.

Reviewing the entire scenario a conclusion can be drawn that there is considerable scope for achieving energy security provided there are technical/technological improvements, financial incentives, policy initiatives and willingness to implement and enforce rules and regulations.

EIGHT

ENERGY CONSERVATION: Catalytic Role of Industrial Associations

S. RAGHUPATHY

There is a vast energy saving potential of 20 to 25 per cent. This has been confirmed by several organisations. Now, if this huge saving has to be achieved, there is need to have many energy players. That means there are thousands and thousands of answers required to achieve this national saving. Here the industries' association can also emerge as a major player, and it has vital catalytic role in achieving national energy savings. In this context there are certain advantages of the role of industries association. I would like to mention some of the points.

First, the main goal of the industries' association is the betterment of the industry. In other words, now the industry can prosper by international competition. Second, is in terms of making propaganda of any National Energy Conservation Activity (NECA).

The industries' association is in an ideal position because it does not avoid network of international and national agencies etc. Second, each industries' association has a wide network of members; and each member is a specialist in itself. So, it has got a wide network of expertise in the form of members. There is a tremendous support there. Needless to say that it also has a high acceptability within the industry. All the top decision-makers are part of industry itself. For any national energy conservation movement to take place, there must be a combination of organisational and technical skills. This is also available with the industries' association. If the national movement has to be successful, this is a very vital element because the organising skills and technical skills are available at one platform. In other words, if you look into all these plus points it is ideally poised for this catalytic role. In other words, all the major industries associations of India can really catalyse and achieve the national objective of energy conservation. They have a major role to play.

I would like to mention, some of the things I initiated and which have been followed up. For example, we are involved in the energy audit. So far about 90 energy audits have been done. These companies have saved over Rs. 18.5 crores within a span of two years. Now, in addition to major areas, there is always a role for many industries' associations to work together. There is a need for standards. There is a need for norms. For example, one major area which has been attempted is developing energy conservation norms for industry. CII has already done some work for paper industry with the Indian Pulp and Paper Technical Association; and cement is being worked out with Cement Manufacturers' Association. There is a tremendous catalytic role here in the sense that norms *per se* are highly debatable. I think, no two engineers can agree on a single figure. If you put two engineers and give them a figure to discuss and arrive at a conclusion and put them separately in a room, they will not come out with conclusions. They will come out only with blows. Norms *per se* have a lot of controversies. But, if you view it in the correct perspective, consider it as an eyeopener and as a benchmark, it has a lot of managerial implications. Industry can take it as a benchmark and try to emulate that. In other words, norms have a tremendous potential. That way, paper industry has been a tremendous success. We are looking forward to the same thing in cement also.

There is a desperate need to create awareness on energy saving devices. Exhibitions provide ideal opportunities to work out these types of programme. So in other words, the industries associations can create awareness.

To mention an example of how the catalytic role of industry associations can really benefit in energy saving, there are companies which have done good work; and in the last five or ten years, savings of about 15 to 20 per cent have been achieved. For example, one company has saved about Rs. 7.35 crores in a span of about three years. So, in other words, a lot of industries are reacting to the energy conservation situations and there is a pinch for price; pinch for the competitive effort. I think, now the trend has very clearly set in, either the company has to do it or it has to get out of business. The writing is on the wall.

Another area of major catalytic role is the formation of ENCON. These ENCON missions, organised by the industries associations, are very effective. When I say ENCON mission, it can be within India or abroad. The concept is that members from all over India will be selected and will be taken to energy efficient companies. They will be exposed to various energy conservation measures that have been undertaken. In other words, seeing is believing. If you see good things being done, one tends to copy it or one tends to develop on it further and implement it in other factories. In other words, major savings can be catalysed by these ENCON missions. CII is able to break the competitive barrier and bring in all people so that they can share information and they can acquire knowledge and, later on, they can implement it in their area. In other words, we see a tremendous benefit, the success rate is very high and this has got a tremendous national benefit.

Coming back now to the major area in terms of the macro level approach of energy conservation, one interesting observation has been going on for the last two to three years. The characteristics of some of the good companies as to how they were able to achieve something like 20 to 50 per cent energy conservation in a span of three years can be visualised from the following. Specific energy consumption is the main parameter for highlighting energy savings. So, reduction in specific energy consumption speaks for itself. If you agree on reduction in specific energy consumption as the main criteria of success, then, there are three fundamental ways of achieving this. To achieve reduction in specific energy consumption at a macro level, the first major area is increasing production. For, maximising the capacity utilisation of the factory leads to tremendous benefits. One can argue that this is not a pure form of energy conservation. But, it gives a tremendous saving. In 80 per cent of the companies the reason for affecting savings upto 20 per cent is the increase in production. India is right now, increasing capacity utilisation or increasing production and has a tremendous benefit not only in energy, but also for production improvements leading to a reduction in fixed costs, so there is a tremendous increase in profitability. In fact, financial returns of the energy projects have also become very attractive, if they are combined with the effect of production increases. Every year it is not possible to reduce ten per cent. But, increasing the production and thereby optimising the energy inputs has the unlimited scope. Even 20 per cent becomes very small. It can even be 50 per cent.

The second is the fine tuning which is being practised all over India and there is a scope of five to ten per cent saving of energy.

Needless to say that technology upgradation is the major area and here it can give a quantum jump of something like 20-50 per cent. In these two areas we are really not talking of major investments. Probably here there might be some major investment. But in the fine tuning we are talking of investment in few lakhs. In case of technology upgradation, we are straightaway talking in crores.

Coming back to my earlier points, if you see any one of the successful companies, they have adopted all the three approaches. That means, a three-pronged approach within the factory has been adopted. There are three separate teams which are working in tandem to achieve this result and they have a common objective of maximising production, reducing investment cost and cutting down the operating cost.

ROLE OF R&D AND ENERGY AUDIT INSTITUTIONS

NINE

ROLE OF RENEWABLE ENERGY TECHNOLOGIES IN INDIAN ENERGY SCENARIO

VED MITRA, ASHVINI KUMAR and NARENDRA SINGH

In India, the Ministry of Non-Conventional Energy Sources is implementing wide ranging programmes on different aspects of renewable energy sources including the grid quality power generation by wind energy, small hydro, co-generation, bio-mass combustion and solar energy. The Solar Energy Centre, which is an integral part of the Ministry has been established for playing an important role in the development and promotion of solar energy devices/systems in the country.

Role of Renewable Sources of Energy

The renewable sources of energy are environmentaly benign, and represent indigenous energy sources. Biogas, biomass, solar, wind, ocean thermal power, tidal power, sea wave power comprise a widely distributed resource base that can be used for sustainable development. Utilising renewable energy sources is specially valuable in rural and remote areas where the majority of population lives. The people living in these areas do not have access to distribution networks to connect them to large scale centralized energy supply systems, and the increase in population further increases their poverty. Utilizing these sources can provide training, employment and development opportunities that would not otherwise be available. The scale of facilities for manufacturing and assembling renewable energy technologies is usually modest as compared to that of conventional energy sources.

By reducing the demand for fossil fuels, the utilisation of renewable energy sources can result in important benefits in the area of environment, developing security and employment. The reduction in fossil fuel consumption lessens energy supply vulnerability, and would also improve the balance of payment problems in view of the reduction in oil imports.

Potential

India is blessed with abundant supply of renewable energy resources. The estimated potential of renewable energy sources in the country is given in Table 9.1.

TABLE 9.1: **Estimated Potential of Renewable Energy Sources in India**

Source/Technology	Estimated Potential
Biogas Plants	12 million
Biomass	17,000 MW
Improved Chulha	120 million
Solar Energy	5×10^{15} Kwh/year
Small Hydro	10,000 MW
Wind Energy	20,000 MW
Ocean Thermal	50,000 MW
Sea Wave Power	20,000 MW
Tidal Power	9,000 MW

Sectors of Utilization

The utilization of the renewable energy technologies is listed according to the conventional market sectors in Table 9.2.

Solar Energy Centre

The Solar Energy Centre (SEC) is an integral part of the ministry of

TABLE 9.2: **Sector of Utilization**

S.No.	Sector	Sources/Technologies
1.	Domestic: Cooking	Biogas, Improved Chulha, Solar Cookers
2.	Domestic: Heating, Cooling and Lighting	Solar Passive, Solar Active, Solar Photovoltaics, Biogas
3.	Power Generation	Wind, Mini-Micro Hydro, cogeneration, Waste Recycling, Solar Photovoltaic, Biomass based technologies, Ocean Thermal, Tidal, Sea Waves, Geothermal, Fuel cells
4.	Industry: Process Heat	High temperature solar collectors, Biomass energy Systems, Geo Thermal Systems
5.	Transport	Alternate Fuels: Battery Operated Vehicles, Alcohol - Petrol operated Diesel vehicles, Compressed Natural Gas fuelled Vehicles, Hydrogen operated vehicles.

Non-Conventional Energy Sources (MNES) dedicated to the development and promotion of solar energy technologies in India. The Centre functions from its own campus on the Gurgaon-Faridabad road at Gwal Pahari near Delhi.

The principal objectives of the Centre are to undertake design, testing, standardization and training activities relating to both solar thermal and solar thermal photovoltaic technologies. The Centre functions as the national body for the testing and certification of solar energy products. It is also to function as a national facility for solar energy information compilation and dissemination. The Centre coordinates cooperation in the field of solar energy among the Group of 15 (G-15) developing countries and participates in other international activities. It is being developed as a centre of excellence of international standing.

Facilities

The Centre possesses several state-of-the-art facilities for carrying out various activities. These include solar thermal and photovoltaic test facilities, well-equipped workshop for proto-type development, satellite-based communication links and a guest house. The details of some of these facilities are given below:

Solar Thermal Test Facility

The Centre for several years has been carrying out testing of solar collectors, solar cookers and other devices in an outdoor test area. A large area sun simulator and indoor-outdoor test rig have been established recently with assistance from the Government of the Federal Republic of Germany. The facility is established by Dornier GmbH, Germany. This facility enables the testing of full size solar collectors and materials used in them. Overall, the facility is the only one of its kind in South and South East Asia, and is specially suited for developmental and certification testing as per national and international standards.

A calibration lab has been established for pyranometers and thermo-sensors (RTDs and thermo-couples). The method employed for the calibration of pyranometer uses a pyrheliometer as the reference radio-meter, and follows ISO/DP 9846 for producing calibration constant. The calibration of thermo-sensors is performed by using sophisticated and computer controlled instrumentation. The reference sensor is a standard Pt-25 (Model 909-25.5) procured from M/s Isothermal Technology Ltd., England. The reference sensor is calibrated as per national measurement accreditation service, England. The range of temperature in which calibration can be carried out is from room temperature to 430°C.

The Solar Energy Centre has been actively involved in establishing national standards for solar cookers and solar flat plate collectors which have been published by the Bureau of Indian Standards. The Centre is the first institution to be accredited by the BIS to carry out testing as per these standards. One of the important roles of the Centre is to act as the national (referal) test centre for coordinating various testing activities within the country and to develop and update national standards based on the experience generated in this regard.

Solar Photovoltaic Test Facility

A comprehensive photovoltaic (PV) test facility has been established under a project assisted by the United States Agency for international Development. The facility has equipment for accurate measurements on solar cells and PV modules as well as environmental chambers for conducting tests on modules. An infra-camera for detection of hot spots and array testers for outdoor measurements are also available. There are assorted instruments for testing batteries, BOS components and systems. The facility consists of several modern and sophisticated instruments like sun-simulator (Spire Corporation, USA), XT-10 Solar Cell Tester, Portable Data Logging and Acquisition Systems, etc.

A 4 KW PV power plant and a shallow well water pumping facility have also been established during 1993-94 to enable testing of components used in such systems. The Centre is carrying out regular testing of solar lanterns and small lighting systems.

In order to enable a complete characterization of the cells, a spectral response measurement system is being added with the cooperation of the Indian association for the Cultivation of Science, Calcutta. Separately, the solar cell measurement system is being upgraded by connecting it with a computer. This work is being done in association with Indian Institute of Technology, Delhi. Very shortly, an UV Exposure System will also be commissioned at SEC to enable testing of modules under exposure of ultra-violet radiation and studying the effect on the power output and other parameters.

Solar Thermal Power Generation

Prominent options for solar thermal power generation are: parabolic trough systems, central receiver system and dish based system. These three options are at various stages of technological development, and have respective merits. The Solar Energy Centre is considering the idea of technology assessment, R&D and demonstration in the field of solar thermal power generation with an aim to help the country in this important area.

Daylight Measurement Station

India is participating in the International Daylight Measurement

Programme with the Central Building Research Institute, Roorkee coordinating the activity. A Research Station for this purpose is being established at Roorkee with financial support from the Department of Science and Technology and CSIR. As part of the national programme, the Solar Energy Centre will also be establishing a general station for measurement of daylight parameters. The data generated at SEC will be of use to architects and designers in the Delhi area interested in the construction of buildings which optimise the use of daylight. The station at Gwal Pahari is expected to be operational before October-November, 1995.

Services Offered by the SEC

The following services are offered by the SEC to the industry and other interested organizations:

- testing of solar collectors and solar cookers as per national and international specifications.
- calibration of pyranometers and thermo-sensors.
- testing of solar cells and photovoltaic modules under standard conditions.
- testing of solar lanterns and other photovoltaic systems.
- advisory and consultancy services for the design of solar thermal systems.
- solar energy database and information network.
- training programmes and seminars.

Conclusion

In view of the vast potential of renewable energy sources in the country, it appears imperative to overcome shortages of energy by conserving it and by developing and adopting renewable energy technologies. The Solar Energy Centre is already active in this field, and solicit the cooperation of all concerned specially the industry and users. To conserve energy and development of renewable sources of energy may be a matter of education today, but, present day consciousness would bear fruit at a later date.

TEN

DAYLIGHTING: A Simple Way of Energy Conservation

D.P. KOTHARI

A discussion on energy conservation normally centres around the argument that 1 MW saved is 1 MW generated. I would like to insist that 1 MW saved is almost 2.5 MW generated when we consider the effect of plant load factor and transmission and distribution losses. One aspect of the grid supply is T&D losses. These can be avoided if focus in generation and supply is shifted from grid power systems to decentralised systems.

In a lighter vein people say that even if a transmission line passes through a village, they declare it to be electrified. So for those 15 per cent villages left out where transmission line is also not passing, we should consider different renewable energy sources—micro and mini hydel, wind, solar, and integration of all of them as these are all proven technologies and are commercially viable. There is going to be 2000 MW of wind and about 1000 MW mini and micro hydel in India.

It is nice to think in terms of different time zones. India can have 4 time zones where a time differential of half-an-hour can be introduced. Such zoning will be helpful when the national grid takes shape. Peaks in different zones will be staggered and the peaking shortage will be avoided. At present 20 per cent shortage is reported. Zoning may bring it down to about 5-6 per cent. The 15 per cent difference will mean saving an installed capacity of 15,000 MW. Even if we consider present investment of Rs. 4 crores per MW, an expenditure of R. 60,000 can be avoided.

The second is saving by effective use of daylight. For example, in summer if you can shift the clock by one hour. As it is if I ask my students to come at 7 o'clock nobody will come. But you make 7 o'clock into 8 o'clock then psychologically everyone is ready to come. By the time our office hours are over or working day is over at 4 o'clock, a lot of time is left in the evening for other activities. That is another possibility of energy conservation.

ELEVEN

ENERGY CONSERVATION IN INDIA: Some Issues

SARTAJ S. MATHUR

While it is true that total availability of energy in India is much less than desired, it is equally true that the use of energy, all across the board, is rather inefficient. If efforts are made to improve the efficiency of energy use, the presently available energy can effectively be increased by at least 25 per cent. To appreciate this possibility, one only has to recall that western countries in the wake of the first energy crisis in 1973 were able to effect 20-40 per cent savings in energy in different sectors. Apart from discovery of more oil, this was an important factor to contribute to the oil glut in the 80s.

Western countries have always been at the forefront of technical knowledge. If they could make improvements resulting in so much of energy savings, the scope for the same in India is considerably greater. This is particularly feasible in the current economic and industrial scenario in the country because of much greater scope and opportunities to utilise modern technology and know-how, as well as, responsive attitude of the industry.

Components of Energy Conservation

Conservation of energy can be effected at each stage of energy production, conversion, transportation and utilisation. The methodology and the scope, however, would depend upon the energy resource, types of technologies utilised and the manner in which the operations are managed.

A very important parameter for deciding on the adoption of energy conservation technologies is the financial investment required and the cost benefit analysis of the proposed technology or changes to be introduced. Equally important is the relative pay-back period for the investment required for energy conservation compared to other demands on the financial resources. The subject is very broad and extensive. Possibility of power conservation in industrial sector, including products, and introduction of renewable energy sources have been considered below:

Power Sector

This is a sector with maximum scope for improvement. The machinery and the technology to produce electricity in a number of power plants is totally outdated. There is also a problem of maintenance, sometimes due to lack of spare parts. As a result, the efficiency as well as the plant load factor are extremely low. While some of these plants can be upgraded or modernised, some other need to be scrapped. The investment required for upgradation of plants is much lower than for putting up new plants. Routine housekeeping and optimisation of performance of sub-systems can yield better performance of existing plants.

The other area of great concern is the heavy loss of power in transmission and distribution. Internationally, these losses amount to less than 10 per cent. In India, in some of the states, the figure is as high as 45 per cent with a national average of about 22 per cent. There is a great scope for savings on this account but the remedy is not entirely technical. The proportion of power stolen by industrialists, agriculturalists and domestic users is quite high even in metropolitan cities like Delhi. Control of this widespread practice requires political decision and strict enforcement.

Industrial Use Sector

The industry has the maximum challenge for saving energy. This can be done through:

(i) adoption of more efficient technologies,

(ii) utilisation of waste heat in industrial processes,
(iii) biomethanation of industrial effluents, and
(iv) utilisation of industrial waste biomass.

While the first option may be capital intensive, the other three offer very attractive opportunities, not only in terms of fast pay-back of investment, but also in terms of environment and pollution control. Sugar, pharmaceuticals, paper and pulp, breweries, textile, chemical, fertiliser and processing industries are some of those industries which have the best scope to adopt these strategies.

Equipment, Devices and Appliances

For a large country like India, items of common use, for example, light bulbs, fans (all types), pumps, electronic goods, domestic appliances etc., aggregate to a high proportion of the total energy consumption in the country. There has been considerable development in regard to design, use of material and manufacturing of these items and the modern gadgets are relatively less energy consumptive than the earlier ones. It is expected that in the new environment of liberalised economy and India wanting to become an important member of the global society, the industry will soon adopt, on a competitive basis, new methods of production and bring in the market equipment, appliances and devices which are not only cheap but energy/efficient as well as durable. The potential of resultant saving in energy is extremely large.

Renewable Sources of Energy

Though use of renewable sources of energy does not save energy in the strict sense, this step certainly reduces the consumption of fossil fuels like, coal, gas and oil. Since renewable sources of energy, a priori, are not depletable these sources can be used for ever and help in increasing the availability of fossil fuels for use where renewable sources cannot be utilised.

During the last two decades, a number of technologies, utilising renewable sources of energy have been developed. Some of these are also economically viable. Some others are attractive in view of the non-availability of any other sources of energy in remote and hilly areas. Yet another reason to use renewable sources of energy, to the extent possible, is the fact that their use does not result in environmental pollution.

Photovoltaic systems for lighting, water pumping and refrigeration, solar thermal systems for providing hot water and steam for domestic and industrial applications, solar dryers, desalination units and cookers are well known applications of solar energy. Similarly, use of wind energy for power generation, pumping and to provide shaft power utilisation of water falls and running waters to generate mechanical and electrical power are some of the options which have reached a stage of technical development and reliability to offer strong alternatives to fossil fuel based systems.

Conclusion

There is an enormous potential to effect savings in conventional power generation, transmission and use in industrial production sector. At the same time, use of modern technology can cut down the consumption of power and improve the efficiency of various devices and appliances. In addition, use of renewable sources of energy, particularly in remote and hilly regions, can mitigate the problem of energy shortages to a significant extent. Thus, a policy of energy conservation and renewable energy use can be beneficial to the country.

TWELVE

SOLAR DISH POWER GENERATION: Technology of Conservation

N.D. KAUSHIK

The specific problem: the problem which relates to energy conservation in developing countries with reference to India, is that Indian energy consumption pattern is rather unique in the world.

Countries like the United States and Japan have noted that energy consumption is a scientific function of management, and through their pragmatic policies and other management strategies they have been able to cut down their energy consumption. We can draw some lessons from their experience. In our country Petroleum Conservation Research Association, (PCRA), is doing a good job. They have found out various methods through management and pragmatic policies to cut the consumption of energy in different sectors.

The long term approach for energy conservation in a country like India must involve either the introduction of new processes or new technologies. I give an example of a new technology that relates to the renewable energy utilization and illustrates to you as to how it can help in energy conservation. This technology is the parabolic solar dish technology. We can produce high temperature and preserve heat. Parabole dishes are arranged in an array and they are used for power generation. In recent years it is generally felt that this parabolic dish technology is very costly. This technology is centre stage. This is a sophisticated technology and this is not the costliest.

In recent years, such developments have taken place that technologists have been able to make two axes striking parabolic dishes of 300 square metres. This is just one single dish where the parabolic character has been simulated. This generates high temperature steam that is used for the generation of power. This just one single simulated dish is able to produce 50 KW of power. It can very well be operated in a country like India, a parabolic dish is being fabricated here by a village level worker.

In the rural sector we have large amount of agro-residues and some industries also have wastes. But that waste is never sufficient to feed a turbine of say some MW range. Also, the agro residue is available in certain seasons and not in other seasons. We can always hybridise parabolic dish with such a thing.

THIRTEEN

ENERGY CONSERVATION IN AGRICULTURE PUMPING SYSTEMS

KULDIP SINGH SAYANN, VISHNU PRASAD and NAGRAJ SITARAM

The pumps used for lift irrigation in agriculture sector consume a large part of energy. At present about 17 per cent of the total energy consumption is accounted for by the agriculture sector. Out of this, about 85 per cent energy is consumed by pumping systems used for lift irrigation. There are about 120 lakh pumping systems used for lift irrigation; and 10 lakh pumping systems are added every year. Out of these systems about 64 lakh are operated by electric motors and the rest are operated by diesel or petrol engines. Most of the pumps used in agriculture sector are observed to run inefficiently.

The surveys and studies conducted so far reveal that the pumping systems operated by the farmers of our country are inefficient. The approximate consumption of electricity or diesel in such pumping systems is 150 per cent to 200 per cent of the required level of consumption. Such excessive consumption of electricity or diesel can be, and should be, reduced so as to avoid the difficulties due to shortage of energy and power in our country. This can be achieved at a very low cost.

Agricultural Pumping Systems

The pumping system consists of the following elements:

(i) Pumps, generally centrifugal pumps which impart energy

to water flowing through impeller by centrifugal action.

(ii) Prime movers, may be either electrically operated motors or diesel/petrol engines and supply energy to pumps.

(iii) Piping system consisting of suction and delivery pipes.

To identify problem areas each one of the components needs to be carefully studied.

Main Causes for Low Overall Efficiency of Pumping System

Following main causes have been observed:

(i) Low efficiency of the pump and the prime mover.

(ii) High specific fuel consumption of the engine.

(iii) Improper selection of pump and prime mover.

(iv) Excessive power losses in power transmission from prime mover to pump.

(v) Improper installation.

(vi) Poor suction lift characteristics (NPSH) of the pump.

(vii) High friction losses in the foot valve and piping system.

(viii) Air leakage in suction pipe.

(ix) Improper maintenance due to wrong spares and lack of service facilities.

Suggested Measures for Energy Conservation in Agricultural Pumping Systems

A large part of energy consumption in pumping system can be saved by taking proper preventive measures as explained below:

Proper Selection of Pumps and Prime Movers

The efficiency of pumps and prime movers has a direct bearing on the energy consumption; higher the efficiency more will be the energy saving. The selection of pumps and its prime mover plays an important role in providing high efficiency. While making the selection of pumps, the complete study of pump characteristics should be made. Most often the pumps are selected without much consideration for head and discharge. Especially in agriculture, purchase is made of inefficient and cheaper pumps.

The selection of prime mover must be made by taking care for starting current, torque and its efficiency. Prime mover starting torque/speed should be well above that of the pump.

TABLE 13.1: **Comparison of Starting Condition of Three Phase Motors**

	Type of Motor	Type of Starter	Starting Current as % of F.L.C.	Starting Torque as % of F.L.T.
(i)	Squirrel (Sq.) Cage	D.O.L.	600	120
(ii)	Double Sq. Cage	D.O.L.	450	215
(iii)	Sq. Cage	Star-Delta	200	40
(iv)	Double Sq. Cage	Star-Delta	150	70
(v)	Sq. Cage	Auto Transformer	250	50
(vi)	Double Sq. Cage	Auto Transformer	190	90
(vii)	Slip Ring	Stator Rotor	120	100

It will be observed from Table 13.1 that the lowest starting current values are obtained by slip ring motor. However, wherever possible a squirrel cage motor should be used because of its robustness, simplicity, higher efficiency, lower cost and less maintenance as compared to slip ring motor.

Proper Installation of Pump Sets

It is generally observed that pumps are installed at any location from water level in the well, without taking much care for 'NPSH' characteristics resulting in poor performance of the pump selected. Some of the suggestions for proper installation of pump-sets are given below:

(i) The water level fluctuations in the irrigation well are more and hence care must be taken that the available 'NPSH' is always greater than the required 'NPSH' specified by the manufacturer.

(ii) The pump sets should be properly aligned with the prime mover otherwise it will lead to wastage of energy in friction and create unwanted stresses in the assembly which in turn may damage its parts.

Piping System

The major part of hydraulic energy developed by the pump is lost in piping system due to friction. It is a general tendency of farmers to use cheaper, bad quality and inadequate size of foot valve and pipes resulting in more energy losses. This loss can be minimised by optimum design of piping system and use of good material in manufacturing.

Rectification of Existing Pump Sets

The experts of ICM - Ahmedabad (1995) had developed improved foot valves and low friction RPVC pipes for use in the suction and delivery lines to reduce the friction losses (30% to 35%). Different rectification measures worked out by replacement of piping system, foot valve and inefficient pumps at 6700 sites proved that the energy consumption in agriculture pumps can be reduced by 20 to 60 per cent and it was also found techno-economically feasible.

Improvement in Operating Conditions

Most of the agricultural pumps operate above or below the design values of the parameters (head, discharge etc.) and are also subjected to voltage fluctuations. These variations are beyond control and affects the performance of the system to a large extent. The variable speed pumps respond to the changing condition in much better way than any other control system and reduce power consumption.

Almost all the state electricity boards are short of power supply, proper capacity transformers and distribution systems which in turn leads to overloading. Due to above reasons all pump sets at the tail end get very low supply of voltage at peak load time which invariably results in heavy losses in the system.

It is observed that the alignment of the pump set gets disturbed due to differential settlement of foundation blocks or differential loadings due to faulty piping system resulting in damage of packing seals and bearings. Proper maintenance of the overall pumping system must be carried out periodically. A proper wire mesh must be kept around the foot valve at a certain distance to avoid choking of foot valve from debris etc.

Quality Control and Standardisation

An optimum design of pump systems reduces the overall losses to minimum, leading to high efficiency and conservation of energy. A wide range of materials like pig iron, foundry chemicals, steel, copper, bronze etc are used in pump manufacturing process. The use of poor quality and low cost materials will increase the energy losses in the pumping systems. The energy saving due to use of best products in pumping system in place of average low quality products is highlighted in Table 13.2.

It is clear from the Table 13.2 that effective control over the quality of end product can be achieved by controlling the specification at every stage of manufacture of pumps and their accessories, right from procurement of raw materials to packing. Standardisation of manufacturing process will improve the overall performance of the

TABLE 13.2: **Comparative Performance of Best and Average Products**

Sr. No.	Product	Characteristics	Performance		Expected Energy Saving
			Best Product	Average Product	
(i)	Engine	SFC in G/kWH	240-250	270	5-10%
(ii)	Electric	Efficiency	80-85%	75-80%	5-10%
(iii)	Electric monoblock	a) Overall Eff. b) Suction lift	65-70% 7-8.5 m	47-55% 6m	20-40% -
(iv)	Pump	Efficiency	75-78%	55-65%	20-35%
(v)	Footvalve	Friction Coeff.	0.5-0.8	3.0-7.0	8-12%
(vi)	Pipes	Hazen William's Const.	150	120-140	10-15%
(vii)	Total Pumping System	Overall Efficiency	55-60%	25-40%	25-55%

pumping system.

Bureau of Indian Standards

Over a period the Bureau of Indian Standard has brought out a number of standards for the guidance of pump-set manufacturers for agricultural purposes under the Pump Sectional Committee EDC35 and EDC14 etc.; some of them are listed in Table 13.3.

Awareness/Training Camps for Energy Conservation

Training of people at every level on energy conservation is to be

TABLE 13.3: **List of ISI Codes for Pumping System**

IS No.	Title
IS 325	Specification for three phase induction motor
IS 999	Specification for single phase small A.C. and Universal Electronic motors
IS 6595	Specification for horizontal centrifugal pumps for clear, cold and fresh water for agricultural purposes.
IS 7538	Three phase squirrel cage induction motor for centrifugal pumps for agricultural application
IS 8034	Specification for submersible pump sets
IS 9079	Specification for mono-set pumps for clear and cold water for agricultural purposes.
IS 9283	Motors for submersible pump sets.
IS 10061	PVC insulated winding wires for submersible motors.
IS 10804	Recommended pumping system for agricultural purposes.
IS 10805	Specifications for foot valves, reflex valves, non-return valves and bore valves used in suction lines of agricultural pumping systems.
IS 11170	Performance requirement for constant speed compression ignition diesel engine for agricultural purposes up to 20 KW.
IS 11346	Specification for testing setup for agricultural pumps (under revision).
IS 11501	Engine monoset pumps for clear, cold and fresh water for agricultural purposes.
IS 12225	Specifications for jet centrifugal pump combination.

accomplished starting from the officers of Government of India; personnel in state electricity boards, state marketing federation, banking institutions, block level officers, dealers and farmers.

Massive training and demonstration for use of energy efficient pumping system and their maintenance has to be carried out at block/ village level which will help in motivating the people at various levels to go for efficient system. Extensive publicity is to be made at the national level through advertisement on Doordarshan, video shows, radio, cinema slides etc. The direct users of the 'Energy Efficient Pumping System' are the farmers and they are interested in monetary gains. Therefore, they must be explained in effective manner the advantages in terms of money saving by the use of good quality pumps and pipes in the long run.

Conclusion

Following specifc points can be concluded:

(i) There is a large scope of energy conservation in pumps used in the agriculture sectors.

(ii) The energy consumption of existing pump sets alone can be reduced by 20 to 60 per cent taking into account the factors such as minimising friction losses, using variable speed pumps, avoiding misalignment of pump sets etc.

(iii) The pump should be manufactured with strict quality control at every stage, starting from procurement of raw materials to installation and commissioning as per IS Codes (Table - 13.3).

(iv) The pump should be designed so as to get top flat efficiency curve as there is a large variation of head and discharge.

(v) Awareness/training camps for energy conservation should be arranged regularly at grass-roots level. Wide publicity about energy efficient system should be done on Doordarshan National Network.

(vi) Continuous research in the area of energy conservation in pumps should be monitored and should be incorporated in the IS Codes to improve performance of pumping systems.

FOURTEEN

ROLE OF NATIONAL PRODUCTIVITY COUNCIL IN ENERGY CONSERVATION

S. KITTAPPA

A major problem that we face as far as energy conservation objectives are concerned is that energy really has not become the priority of the end user, to the extent that it should have. We discussed about the gap in our projected demand for 2006-07. Adding the load factor of our own 60 per cent, it is frightening to think about the magnitude of the capacity to be added in this country in the next ten years. Government has been acting in the right direction during the current Five Year Plan—a target of 5000 MW has been kept for energy saving. Organisations like EMC are already working in this area. The reason being that the cost of saving is much lees than the cost of generation of equivalent power. Organisations like National Productivity Council and many other consultancy agencies and individuals are working towards the energy saving assisting industries in many ways.

First is helping them through energy audit and conservation measures.

Second is the development of sector or sub-sector specific energy norms. This is an area where we may have to work a lot because quite many of the problems which we have discussed earlier could be solved if norms could be developed.

Third area where some efforts could be put is the demand side management. NPC takes up studies on 'demand side management' for the state as a whole. It starts with the conservation study to see how the industries can reduce their real consumption. Initially through good house-keeping which can be a short-term measure and can be immediately attended to and some results can be realised by the end user. The other could be energy efficient techniques studying different operations, methods of operation, their maintenance system and also the equipment used and so on; and coming out with some suggestions, small modifications which really not change the technology *per se*. This could be an immediate measure or could have a pay-back period of one to two years and industries are readily forthcoming to implement such measures. The third level is going in for energy efficient technologies. Very often, consultants have some difficulty here because of the lack of availability of information regarding which technology will really be suitable to the current situation. Also, if it is cost intensive the organisations (the end-users) may have to have a long drawn plan for shifting or changing from one level of technology to another level of technology. Under the Demand side management, the other area where we can concentrate is reducing the peak time demand. Again through the energy audit it can be identified and the end users can be assisted to reduce their own peak demand by distributing the load and so on. Finally, taking an area or a state as a whole or a cluster where energy efficient industries are located different aspects can be studied. How to distribute their peak demand? Whether they can have some arrangement amongst themselves or any other time difference of operations can be introduced so that the peak demand can be reduced in the area so that we may have more power available for usage of others? It could also call upon developing modules for sub-sectors of energy intensive industries like steel plants, rolling mills, paper plants and so on.

There is also a policy level decision which could be initiated or where it can be generated for the policy bodies to deliberate and find out whether it could be introduced by dual pricing. Dual pricing, because we have different pricing for energy during the peak demand period and for the rest of the lean period. This can be a punitive measure or an incentive measure.

FIFTEEN

ENERGY ANALYSIS IN AGRICULTURE AND ANIMAL HUSBANDRY

A.R. RAO

India is bothered about the energy efficiency of various kinds of foods; for instance for the various crops and the animal products. The general impression has been that we have a lot of useless cattle; so get rid of them; let us enjoy the beef. But that appears to be a very short-sighted situation. Then we went deeper into the whole problem. The source of all energy at present, and also from the pre-historic time has been Sun. Only 1.2 per cent of the energy falling on the earth is stored in plants. About 99 per cent is the waste. Same is applicable to crops, natural heritage and trees with small variations between the present varieties of plant matter. The crops again have about 0.4 per cent in the form of grains and about 0.8 per cent in the form of by-products. The by-products have diverse uses; they can go into making charcoal or directly as fuel or they can also be used for other industries like paper. In our country the by-products have been a great source of sustenance for the entire livestock industry. For instance, without the use of crop residues we could not have had any animal husbandry in this country. This accounts for about 70 per cent of all the energy intake of animal husbandry. And in other countries where they don't have this kind of tradition, like in the US, crop residues are the biggest source of pollutants in the biosphere. So, the pollutants in one country become a vital resource for an entire industry in this country. The main product, the grains, can also go into livestock; as also the natural herbage. Livestock can be used to work on farms or give foods like milk and meat which again go to man and man puts out work. Dung from livestock can be used as a fuel or manure.

Firewood from the trees can be used as fuel and wasted energy of the sun is the thermal energy which is sufficiently cheap to trap and very much more expensive in the form of photovoltaic conversion. Our studies on agriculture, particularly in Haryana have shown that the major inputs into crop production have been in the form of farmyard manure and irrigation-mainly canal irrigation; and bullocks and farm equipment. All these are non-commercial materials.

If you do the accounting of energy inputs in agriculture as they do in western agriculture, we come to the conclusion that on rainfed farms there are absolutely no inputs and what you get is only the output as a little grain and crop residues. We did accounting from the primary fuel wastage. For example, from farmyard manure we valued it as the thermal energy value of farmyard manure; not as the energy equivalent of nitrogen, phosphate and potassium which are the fertilizers in farmyard manure. In that way we found that, if you want to supply this NPK as fertilizers, the input will hardly be 5 or 6 per cent of what it would be as farmyard manure. In other words we are wasting about 95 per cent of the energy of farmyard manure if we are using it as a source of NPK. It is much more worthwhile to use the fertilizers directly and save the farmyard manure to be used as perhaps simple dung cakes by the poor who need badly some fuel everyday for their cooking.

Most of the farms are small; and so there is an excess of power which is not being utilised. In other words even if you have got a pair of bullocks they are not sufficiently used because the land does not require them. Bullock operated farms are observed to be much more expensive even in terms of monetary costs.

Several common assumptions on energy use in agriculture were verified using physical input-output parameters obtained from agro-economic data of Haryana and transformed into energy equivalents. The method of process analysis was applied to evaluate energy utilisation in agriculture. Major inputs were identified as those derived through farm yard manure (FYM), irrigation, bullocks and farm equipment. Farm surveys were conducted to study these inputs. Inputs were computed from the stage of primary fuel, like coal for electricity; iron ore and fabrication for mechanised equipment; energy embodied in bricks and cement for irrigation; food and fodder for labour and livestock towards bullock power.

Tubewell irrigation consumed 9,274 MJ for a hectare of wheat. Energy inputs for irrigation formed 6.8 per cent of the energy output from the main product of sorghum fodder, 13.9 per cent of berseem, 15.2 per cent of wheat, 15.9 per cent of sugar, 118.8 per cent of cotton and 37.0 per cent of rice. Total energy inputs were 249 to 324 MJ per cm.ha in different crops. Bricks form a major energy input in irrigation systems.

Fully utilised, the minimum energy inputs through equipment for a hectare of wheat would be of 9.2 GJ on bullock-operated farms and 5.9 GJ on tractor-operated farms. Actually, due to small size, they use 29.2 GJ on bullock-powered farms and 8.3 GJ on those with tractors. Monetary costs of wheat production are about 40 per cent higher on bullock-operated farms. Chemical pest and weed control account for about 3 per cent of the energy input of crops.

Energy returns as grain are 99 per cent for wheat, 90 per cent for dwarf rice, 76 per cent for Basmati rice and 17 to 28 per cent for maize and as sugar 52 per cent in planted and 103 per cent in ratooned sugarcane. A crop rotation of paddy and wheat in Haryana, on an annual basis, consumes less energy and yields more energy in the edible form and as biomass, than a crop of sugarcane. Total energy conversion efficiency for a cotton crop is 28.7 per cent and for cotton fibre, 25.2 per cent.

Rural fuel supplies being marginal, dung is preferentially used as fuel and hardly 10 per cent of the recommended levels of FYM are applied. Energy utilization from dung as fuel is double that as fertilizer replacement. Due to capital costs, biogas will not be the fuel of the poor. *Gobar* gas will force the poor to fell vegetation for cooking fuel.

Indian agriculture appears to account for most of the national consumption of energy (mainly non-commercial). Considering the extensive, daily needs for low-or no-cost cooking fuel, it is concluded that the overall energy economy of the country as well as that of agriculture will improve by encouraging the use of fertilizers and minimising the use of FYM, as well as farm and transport mechanisation (by reduced dependence on bullocks).

Conclusion

We have the situation where about 41 per cent of the energy in the country is coming from non-commercial sources and we are largely ignoring this sector in our energy conservation planning.

SIXTEEN

EXPERIENCES IN ENERGY CONSERVATION

CHARLES FAFARD

Our company has been involved here in India for the last year and a half on the MKF project. And I should also mention that we are working in association with the IDBI as our local counterpart. In the last two and a half years that we have been here. I have made certain observations that I would like to share with you.

Identification of Potential Energy Saving Energy Activities Not Done

Firstly, in association with Indian consultants, we have done what we call preliminary audits into the cement, the fertilizers, papers, sponge iron industry and commercial airconditioned buildings. Our engineers and the Indian consultants together in a day and half, in essence, were able to go into a plant and talk with the operating personnel in the management of the plant and find probably four to six energy conservation items that have very attractive pay backs, that have been implemented. The bottom line of this is that everybody knows that these items are there. But they just haven't taken time to identify and assign numbers to them. They are not aware what the paybacks are? But, they are there and these are very real projects.

Role of Energy Manager

In one facility we identified an Energy Manager. But, we found that in fact, that position or that person is not what we, classically in US, call Energy Manager from the conservation point of view. In India, the Energy Manager is trying to make sure that there is power or there is power available once the processes are operating. And the focus is totally different from energy conservation. I don't plead that any one of those facilities that we have visited have in fact graphed in their consumption on a monthly basis compared year to year to try to see if they were able to make improvement. I believe there is a need for an association of Energy Managers in India similar to what we have in the US.

Legislative Measures

Another point I would like to discuss is legislation. When we look at the activities in US what we really see is whether a legislation on many factors of the energy efficient equipment produce an equipment within a certain efficiency range. If they are not going to produce high efficiency equipment, then there should be a tax on lower efficiency equipment. Motors typically consume 60-70 per cent of industrial energy. In some of the activities it was observed that in replacement of motors in industrial environment, most of the time people would go for rewinding and in the rewinding shops of motors there is absolutely no control or no certification. So, what you get might probably be worse than what you bought except hat it works. Now the real efficiency is not in the right direction. So, may be, there should be an attempt to certify more rewinders.

Energy Labelling

A third point, somewhat related, would be the labelling of equipment. In the US it is mandatory to put energy label on each equipment. The airconditioners and a lot of other industrial products have a label right on top of the equipment that will show that for a usage what will be the rate of power consumption and/or what the cost would be for that particular unit. I think, labelling of equipment would be a benefit in many ways.

Demand Side Management

Under the USAID Project, we are working with Ahmedabad Electric Company in establishing demand side management, DSM, for their industrial customers. This is just underway and I can tell you that they have been able to achieve a great amount of KW demand savings. In fact, there are several areas that are targeted and we are planning to take the workshops around to other utilities in trying to encourage the demand side management. But, one of the things would be to motivate utilities to implement demand side management.

Law for Imported Equipment

Another point for consideration is the law for imported equipment. There is already shortage of certain types of energy audit equipment in this country, that does not actually meet the standards that we have in US. We try to get our equipment that will provide energy efficiency. But we find the deterioration during operation is 25 to 100 per cent. That kind of thing is counterproductive to energy efficiency also. I would like to see that ESCOs are encouraged. We are trying to do that, but I can tell you that this is actually very slow in developing. Again people don't want to get involved in it, because of large cost of implementation of projects. But we are working with the IDBI and some private enterprises to try to develop and implement some ESCOs activities.

Several participant, referred to energy conservation activities in various countries and how appropriate those measures are, I would just like to comment on that. Let me emphasise that it seems to me that our countries, the industrialised countries, are different from developing countries; and certainly the problems are also of different nature. The biggest problem here in India is not energy efficiency necessarily, but the shortage of energy. And when we go into operation of utilities they don't really necessarily talk about energy efficiency. They want to know as to how they can get power to operate? I think, it is that issue that is blocking the energy efficiency issue.

INSTITUTIONAL FINANCE

SEVENTEEN

ENERGY CONSERVATION FINANCING SCHEME OF IDBI

R.M. GANATRA

Sometime in the beginning of 19th century, (precisely it is 1825) when steam engine was invented and made to roll on rails in England, it was thought to be a step forward in taming the internal energy for use by mankind as a substitute for manual and animal power. However, it was only realised later that such release of energy and other materials into the atmosphere on a large scale would also cause environmental degradation. Since then industrial development has continued to rise at a rapid pace all over the world and is considered to be the barometer of economic progress of the nations. For example, in developed countries, the level of power consumption has increased to 10,000 - 14,000 units per year per capita as against 250 to 270 units per capita in our country. Imagine what would happen if our country increased its energy consumption level to say only 1/10th of the level in developed countries which will mean increasing the level of consumption to 4 times of the present level. All our petroleum reserves will vanish in 20 - 25 years and coal in next 100 years. Not only will there be no conventional fuel left, but the damage caused by the emission of carbon dioxide would be catastrophic.

Growth of Power Sector

Talking about the power sector in India, it has grown considerably in the last four decades, from 1713 MW in 1950-51 to 81,164 MW in 1994-95. Similarly, the gross generation of electricity increased from 7 billion kwh in 1950-51 to 351 billion kwh in 1994-95, recording an average annual growth rate of about 10 per cent during the period. Despite this growth rate, the power sector continues to be beset with chronic power (since independence in 1947). With the generating capacity shortages of the public utilities, the All India power deficit remaining at about 7-9 per cent and peak shortage at 18-20 per cent. As per Central Electricity Authority (CEA), 20,730 MW of new capacity are expected to be added during the 8th Plan Period 1992-97. As against this, the actual capacity addition in the first 3 years i.e. upto March 1995 has been 12,675 MW; and during 1995-96, another 2,162 MW are proposed to be added. Thus, the 8th plan target is unlikely to be met. Indications are that by the year 2005, against a requirement of 1,40,000 MW of the installed capacity, we may have a shortfall of 35,000 to 40,000 MW, implying an across the board deficit of 25-30 per cent and peak deficit of about 40 per cent. In the background of the power crisis looming large over the country amidst severe resource crunch, how do we address the country's power needs?

Let me, even at the cost of repetition, recount certain figures concerning the country's supply side management (SSM) and demand side management (DSM) of power. At present our power average shortage is 11 per cent with peak shortage of 32 per cent, while at the same time, our plant load factors (PLF) are low. There are over 10 power plants which have PLFs of 30 per cent or less. Our T&D losses are 23-24 per cent as against 7-8 per cent in USA/Japan. Addition of further capacity at astronomical costs and (under) utilising the same as we do now would be a criminal wastage of our precious resources. Luckily, there are ways of conserving substantial power by improving our SSM and DSM of power. Studies have shown that a proper SSM and DSM coupled with cogeneration can contribute as much as 30,000 MW of power. It is well known that the cost of saving power this way is 1/5th or even 1/10th of the cost of setting up additional capacity. Energy conservation can be pursued by stake holders such as financial institutions, and the supply side bodies (utilities) as a business activity, and by demand side bodies (industry, commerce, and homes) as a cost saving activity.

IDBI's Schemes on Energy Conservation

IDBI recognised the need for energy conservation in industry very early; and since inception, it has been assisting modernisation projects leading to efficient use of energy. I would share with you, IDBI's packages for financing energy conservation projects. However, let me first share with you IDBI's operation. IDBI's sanctions to industry since its inception in 1964 till 31st March 1995, were over Rs. 96,997 crore. The portfolio of IDBI comprises over 3,000 companies across a complete range of industries. IDBI's sanctions in 1994-95 were over Rs. 19,830 crore and disbursements exceeding Rs. 10,620 crore. As on the same date, IDBI's total assets were of the order of Rs. 38,162 crore, and net worth of Rs. 3742 crore. IDBI provides direct and indirect long term loans by way of project finance, equipment finance, equipment leasing, line of credit, bills discounting/rediscounting and refinance of industrial loans. Besides, IDBI has schemes for venture capital financing, pollution control and assistance for energy conservation projects. Assistance is provided in the form of rupee loan, foreign currency loans, underwriting, guarantees and direct subscription to equity. In addition, IDBI provides financial services like merchant banking, debenture trusteeship, forex service, etc. IDBI is also assisting the World Bank in implementing the projects which phase out ozone depleting substances (ODS). The energy conservation/efficiency schemes of IDBI are summarised as under:

Equipment Finance for Energy Conservation (EFEC) Scheme

Under EFEC assistance is given on normal terms for installation of equipment for energy conservation i.e. for building, plant and machinery, miscellaneous fixed assets, erection and installation charges, fees for technical knowhow and fees for drawings and designs.

Energy Audit Subsidy (EAS) Scheme

Under EAS, assistance is provided to the extent of 50 per cent of the cost of the energy audit carried out by approved energy consultants, provided the investment is substantial and commensurate savings are achievable and the company approaches IDBI for financial assistance.

Energy Management Consultation and Training (EMCAT) Project Funded by USAID

In 1991, IDBI started implementing the end-use component of the EMCAT project. The objectives of EMCAT are to improve technological and management capabilities for supply and end-use of energy by industry. Under EMCAT, setting up of demonstration projects, development of energy service companies, cogeneration, drawing up of energy efficiency plans in energy intensive industrial sectors, are visualised with assistance as grants/lines of credit from the international agency. Efforts under EMCAT have resulted in creating wide awareness regarding potential of Indian sugar industry to generate surplus power and has also emphasised SEBs to take advantage of the surplus generating capabilities of the sugar mills. Indian energy auditors are being provided opportunity to improve their skills by learning advanced energy audit techniques internationally used and they are provided with latest instruments for the purpose on cost sharing basis. USAID grant is being used under EMCAT to draw energy conservation/efficiency improvement plans for selected units under the guidance from international experts in power intensive sectors like sponge iron, fertilizer, cement, paper, etc. IDBI has also provided assistance to Demand Side Management (DSM) project by Ahmedabad Electricity Company. IDBI has focused on development of energy service companies (ESCOs) in India by first carrying out a study to determine their feasibility and then financing setting up one ESCO. Similarly, a study was carried out on advancing surplus power generation in Indian sugar industry. Private sugar mills have started setting up facilities for generating surplus power following the change in government policies as a result of widespread publicity to the study and involvement of industry associations.

Under the Loan Portfolio Design (LPD) component of the EMCAT project, preinvestment studies of four energy intensive industrial sectors, viz., cement, fertiliser, paper and sponge iron were initiated in October 1994 by Resource Management Associates of USA, the consortium contractor engaged by USAID under EMCAT. The aim of the studies was to—

* Evaluate the existing process technology and its energy intensity per unit of output.
* Evaluate how "state of the art" technology, as available on the world market, would affect the energy intensity.
* Estimate the simple payback of the financial investments required to implement energy efficient process changes.

The study conducted on four plants each in the above four sectors has indicated that there is a potential for undertaking energy conservation/efficiency projects involving aggregate investments of about Rs. 242 crore, with average payback period of about 5 years. We are looking forward to financing such projects. We hope to replicate this exercise based on our experience.

A 5-year DSM action plan has also been formulated under EMCAT for Ahmedabad Electricity Company (AEC). The objectives of AEC in going in for the DSM action plan were to,

(i) enable AEC to reduce its purchases from GEB (primary).
(ii) be visible to its customers in all major segments.

The exercise has indicated that among the top 8 sector weighted DSM programme options, 5 options are from the industrial (high tension) sector. Therefore, more concentration on the industrial customers, initially is likely to realise the objectives of DSM to a large extent.

Innovative Funding for Saving Energy (INFUSE) Scheme

To assist the industrial units for adopting latest energy conservation techniques and promote energy savings in existing industries, IDBI has introduced INFUSE. It aims at financing energy conservation schemes of industry through performance contracting using shared savings approach for the first time in India. The benefits arising out of the energy saving from the scheme are shared in a predetermined agreed ratio. The methodology of operation is that the industrial unit would get an energy audit carried out by energy consultants and IDBI would fund the capital cost of the scheme to the extent of 80 per cent under INFUSE and determine the ratio in which the benefits arising to the company would be shared by the company, the consultant, and IDBI. The consultant would help the industrial unit for implementing the scheme and monitor energy savings on an ongoing basis. IDBI would monitor the implementation of the scheme and collect its income and recover its dues regularly.

For the purpose of financing specific development projects for energy efficiency purposes IDBI has entered into an agreement with ADB for a line of credit of US $150 million. Under this line of credit, all types of projects will be able to obtain financial assistance for undertaking major projects aimed at improving energy efficiency. The company can avail the assistance either as rupee loan or foreign currency loan. The improvement in energy efficiency across the specific equipment or process should be atleast 18 per cent. The energy actually saved would be measured by energy audit of the company for a period of 5 years after implementation of the project on an annual basis. The company would also have to comply with environmental regulations.

Energy Conservation Possibility in Industry

Studies have shown that India consumes 20-40 per cent more energy in cement, 70-90 per cent in pulp and paper, 20-30 per cent in aluminium and 80-90 per cent in steel plants. The industry as a whole accounts for about 50 per cent of the total electrical energy consumption and is estimated to have a potential to save 15 to 25 per cent through cost effective conservation measures. Thus, the opportunities to reduce energy consumption and improve energy efficiency in the industrial sector are substantial. As we know, energy efficiency also helps in reducing environmental degradation, and provides a competitive edge to the industry. Hence, as an urgent measure, it might be worthwhile to minimise energy consumption in some of the most energy intensive industries such as aluminium, steel, fertiliser, textile, cement, and paper. Most of the energy conservation measures in the industry have payback periods in the range of 1 to 5 years. IDBI would be too glad to extend finance to such viable projects.

Cogeneration in Sugar Industry

The sugar industry is self sufficient in energy, i.e., it uses bagasse for its power and steam requirement. The sugar industry has vast potential for surplus power generation, and it is estimated that efficient cogeneration could yield an additional 3,800 MW of electrical power based on the assumption that Indian mills could generate the same 60-80 kwh per tonne of cane as achieved in Hawaii and borne out in the study on Advancing Co-generation in Indian sugar industry prepared by Winrock International and International Development and Energy Associates under Energy Management Consultation and Training Project.

A recent study conducted by institutions brings out the following major points:

(i) the concept of cogeneration of power is not new to the sugar industry; however, surplus power generation is to a large extent, new to the industry.

(ii) essential pre-requisite for a meaningful co-generation of surplus power in significant quantities is to maximise the energy potential in bagasse and minimise the captive power and steam requirements by use of electrical/hydraulic drives for cane crushing operations and steam economy/ efficient operating practices.

(iii) cogeneration system which operates both during season and off-season is more viable.

(iv) higher average fibre content in cane is preferable. Bagasse should be more than 30 per cent on cane crushed (including 50 per cent moisture) and crushing season should not be less than 160 days.

(v) steam pressure should be as high as feasible under Indian conditions and preferably over 60 kg/square centimeter.

(vi) assured availability of alternate fuels in off season is a must.

(vii) net realisation from the sale of surplus power should not be less than Rs. 2 per unit after wheeling and banking charges are deducted.

(viii) grid system must be compatible and voltage/frequency fluctuations should be minimal.

The above study more or less bears out the conditions stipulated for availing of subsidy for demonstration projects as declared by MNES viz.:

(i) the project should empty bagasse based steam generation of at least 60 kg/sq cm and 450°C.

(ii) the surplus generation must be atleast 5 MW and offer power for sale to SEBs or others for atleast 160 days.

(iii) the mill should have crushed atleast 80 per cent of its installed capacity and recorded net profits for the last 5 years of operations (or if in operation for less than 5 years, then during all the years after commissioning).

(iv) SEB must be willing to wheel/bank/buy-back surplus power generated.

(v) in case of projects which intend to use dual fuel mode of operation subsidy will be given only to the extent bagasse fired capacity on the basis of maximum notional generation of 3 MW for 1000 tcd capacity or as worked out in the detailed appraisal report, whichever, is lower.

It is felt that if various issues mentioned above are resolved, we can utilise the full potential of cogeneration in the sugar industry. To give a fillip to this activity, as also to encourage year round generation of electrical power by the sugar industry through utilisation of alternate biomass fuel during off season, IDBI is implementing yet another USAID programme, viz., Greenhouse Gas Prevention Project (GEEP). The GEEP seeks to assist socially, economically and technically viable and sustainable projects for reducing the volume of emissions of greenhouse gases per unit of energy generated while increasing energy productivity and encouraging biomass fuel use in selected utilities and sugar industries. The Alternative Bagasse Cogeneration (ABC) component of the GEEP project further seeks to provide investment support by way of grant to lower the cost of capital for promoters who design their plants for dedicated usage of alternative biomass fuels.

Conclusion

You would have observed that IDBI has been very active in promoting energy conservation. It has been trying novel methods for promoting energy conservation and improving energy efficiency in industry. The industry must take up energy conservation as a mission and avail of the assistance from IDBI for projects which require large investments.

CONTROL SYSTEMS

EIGHTEEN

CONTROL SYSTEMS FOR ENERGY CONSERVATION IN INDIA

JAY CHATTERJEE and PANKAJ JOSHI

Allen Bradley provides the world's broadest line of control and information technology: More than 350,000 products and product variations all built on the architecture for the future—one that is dedicated to easy integration and interoperability. An architecture that is open at the top to share plant floor data with the computer world and is open at the bottom to companies who make end devices.

We search out and partner with the best producers of specialized technologies and have already partnered globally with more than 140 firms to provide service to a broad spectrum of industries that relies on us for specialized automation solutions: From mining and metals to water and waste water, from pharmaceuticals and food processing to material handling and petrochemicals, from transportation and forest products to plastics and packaged goods.

Specifically for purposes of energy conservation/load management through process improvement, Allen Bradley in India has partnered with leading consultants and process technology suppliers particularly in fertilizer, steel, cement, textile and of late heating, ventilating and air conditioning.

Technology, its Availability and other Issues

In our business, after the economic liberalisation, there is no new technology or new material of general use which is not available to those customers in India (who are concerned about optimum energy use) that is available to their counterparts elsewhere in the world.

From the point of view of new technology absorption, it is very encouraging to note that the recent advances in technology, specially digital electronics and software, have resulted in products that are simple to operate and maintain. The science behind the products may be getting more and more complex every day but the products themselves are getting smarter and transparent so that the user does not need to go into the technical details of the product but only has to concentrate on his process application. Maintenance has been transformed from "repair", with all its requirement of highly skilled people, to "module replacement" by the economics of large scale production coupled with the digital electronics technology. Simplest example is the DC drive - 20 years back commissioning even a small DC drive was a complex exercise. Today Allen Bradley can provide you with drives that are fully automatic with self-tuning capabilities built-in so that commissioning is a matter of filling in menu driven forms. Again, 20 years back a fault in DC drive was enough to make the maintenance people break out into sweat. Today it is no problem—the extensive self-diagnostics of modern drives from Allen Bradley sound the alarm, pin-point the fault in plain English and any reasonably technically literate person can have the fault removed and the drive back on line in a short time by replacing the faulty module. Inverter products were earlier incredibly complex, today Allen Bradley provides you with "plug and play" AC variable frequency drives. The point is that technology assimilation is now no longer a major worrying issue.

Technology has also made products available to a larger spectrum of users. On one end Allen Bradley can provide programmable logic controllers, smart soft starters and AC variable frequency drives in the "micro" and "pico" ranges which enables the small machine manufacturers to produce new efficient products. On the other end we have smart soft starters and AC drives in the very large megawatt range which enable the idling time of large sized equipment to be reduced and also enable them to start without stress on electrical distribution systems.

Data communications technology is a key component in energy management. Various control units—islands of automation—

scattered all over the plant can be linked together and the energy and process data from all sections of the plant can be brought together and transformed into Energy Information which is necessary if the plant Energy Managers are to take informed decisions. Here Allen Bradley provides complete communication technology to deal with two separate but vital issues:

— All Allen Bradley control products have seamless connectivity with each other for exchange of control information and,
— Because a plant may have devices including computers from different vendors, Allen Bradley products provide open connectivity to such devices ranging from programmable serial links to Ethernet TCP/IP connectivity.

An example to illustrate this point would be from Steel Industry where the steel rolling mills would typically use Allen Bradley programmable logic controllers, control co-processors, microprocessor controlled DC and AC drive systems, presence sensors and operator interface devices all seamlessly connected to each other device level (remote I/O) and control level networks and also connected to third party devices like Automatic Guage Control Systems and Weighing Systems for control interlock and process information and to plant host computers for MIS systems.

As the power generation and transmission/distribution systems are privatised we may expect reduction in subsidy to power costs. Power management and use of co-generation and related techniques will therefore become increasingly necessary. We may also expect tighter control and penalties imposed by utilities on maximum demand peaks and power quality as they take steps to increase efficiency as is common practice in other countries. On the user end, increasing use of commutating devices for control of electrically powered equipment will be a major cause of pollution of electric power. It is also not uncommon in other countries to have demand calculations period as short as 5 minutes and even 1 minute. This requires extremely fast response from power management systems. Allen Bradley has a complete Integrated Power Monitoring and

Control solution for this which views power as a process variable to be monitored and controlled. The system would typically consist of intelligent Power monitors with communication facilities and capable of measuring both power variables and power quality variables, programmable logic controllers, operator interface units and associated software.

WEC Council's "Overlooked" Factors—The Unsung Heros of the Energy War

In the course of our deep involvement with the industrial control automation in India we have come to observe the complex nature of the energy consumption itself in industrial processes. There is a very tight coupling between

— methods of process control (manual, degree of automation)
— product quality (just right, no less and with some emphasis—no more!)
— productivity and
— energy consumption.

Allen Bradley believes that introducing automation in processes as a form of process improvement is critical to achieving the right product quality and optimum energy usage. Less quality means rejects which means lowered productivity and waste of energy. More quality may also mean lowering of productivity and resulting energy waste. Our products like Statistical Process Control (SPC) software package enable the quality of the process to be factored in as a process variable to be controlled.

Moreover introducing automation in control of processes and packages like the SPC described above provide the tools to plant personnel to understand their plant behaviour better. This increases the possibility of introduction of new, more efficient, processes with the resulting decrease in energy intensity.

In addition to above, there is a critical issue which the decision makers need to understand. Today's computer technology has made it possible to "capture" the process expert's knowledge and experience and encapsulate it in products that are easy to use by anybody. This is the "great leveller" whch is critical to the "leap frog effect" in the rise of productivity of our country and consequent lowering of energy consumption. A simple example is the Injection Molding package developed by Allen Bradley for the plastics industry. The package contains in itself knowledge of plastics process, as well as the knowledge of advanced PID control, which automatically compensates for errors in the molding machine due to wear and tear, is simple to install, operate and maintain and allows even "lay" users to reap the benefits of increased productivity and product quality while reducing energy consumption.

Technology is making available products for every category of user. We provide today Micrologix 1000, a micro programmable logic controller which is very small in size but with very advanced in features and extremely rugged and reliable. This can be used by small machine manufacturers alongwith our advanced intelligent presence sensors to implement flexible, advanced control schemes to build machines with features for increased efficiency and productivity at costs unimaginable earlier.

Recommendation

As our experience shows, creating an environment in which "doing the right thing" makes economic sense is the only way of sustaining the energy efficiency effort.

Earlier several studies had projected a large rise in use of AC variable speed drives if relief in customs duty and excise duty was provided alongwith help from financial institutions in terms of soft loans for their procurement. This, as our experience shows, is true and further reliefs in the same line would be welcome as it would allow the very latest in technology to come into India.

We would strongly recommend that equipment like PLC, electronic operator interfaces, packaged automation solutions for machines and intelligent power monitoring and control devices be also considered for customs duty exemption and financial help in terms of soft loans and quick depreciation.

ENERGY CONSERVATION EXPERIENCE IN INDUSTRY

NINETEEN

ENERGY CONSERVATION MEASURES IN SAIL

U.K. MITTAL

Energy is a vital input for the growth of industrial sector, which is the largest consumer of commercial energy in the country. In India, this sector is responsible for about 60 per cent of the total commercial energy consumption. The steel industry as a whole is an important energy user as it accounts for nearly 10 per cent of the total energy consumed in the entire nation, to generate about 19 million tonnes of crude steel per annum. Steel production in India is mainly through (i) the Integrated Steel Plants—based on the blast furnace—open hearth/basic oxygen furnace route; and (ii) the Mini Steel Plants—based on scrap or sponge iron—Electric Arc furnace route.

At present, there are seven integrated steel plants in India with an installed capacity of 16.35 million tonnes of crude steel. Five of these seven units are under Steel Authority of India Limited and are located at Bhilai, Durgapur, Rourkela, Bokaro and Burnpur. The other two are Tata Iron and Steel Company at Jamshedpur and Visakhapatnam Steel Plant at Vizag. Apart from this, India also has about 269 Electric Arc furnaces with an annual steel making capacity of 9.3 million tonnes. With the recent changes in the economic policies in India, many new steel plants are also coming up fast.

Energy Consumption Pattern in SAIL

Steel Industry by its very nature is highly energy intensive with its many heating, cooling, melting and solidification cycles. The major energy inputs to the integrated steel unit of SAIL are coking coal, boiler coal, purchased power and petrofuel. Coking coal is the prime fuel for production of blast furnace coke and accounts for about 77 per cent of the total energy input in the steel plant. Boiler coal which is required for steam and power generation in the plant accounts for 13 per cent. Petrofuels meant to compensate for the fuel deficit or special process requirement account for 2 per cent and Purchased power meant for supplementing the captive power generation accounts for 8 per cent of the total energy input to the plant.

The specific energy consumption in an integrated steel plant is computed as per the standardised methodology prescribed by the International Iron and Steel Institute, Brussels. Typically, the specific energy consumption of integrated steel units in SAIL ranges from 7.5 Gcal/tcs to 13 Gcal/tcs. Amongst them, Bhilai Steel Plant has been recording the lowest Specific Energy Consumption for the last few years.

Very often it is stated that the energy consumption level in Indian steel industry is double compared to that in the advanced countries (Table 19.1).

However, such comparisons are often misleading as the figures presented for foreign countries are averages which include electric arc furnace route of steel making also (Table 19.2). The scrap-based EAF method of steel production requires considerably less energy than the integrated route of steel making.

Moreover, in the advanced countries, the steel plants have completely switched over from the Open Hearth route of steel making to more energy efficient BOF route of steel making. Similarly, ingot casting route has been replaced by continuous casting technology (Table 19.3). However, Indian integrated steel units are still continuing with energy inefficient Open Hearth (OH) steel making process where the energy consumption is about ten times compared to the energy consumption in the LDF process.

Energy Conservation in SAIL

The importance of energy conservation as a precondition for economic viability was recognized by SAIL way back in the eighties. SAIL

TABLE 19.1: **Energy Consumption in Steel Industry**

Unit: - Gcal/tcs

Country	Specified Energy Consumption
United Kingdom	4.7
U.S.A.	5.1
Germany	4.8
Japan	4.2
Italy	4.5
Spain	3.8
Sweden	4.7
India	7.5-13

TABLE 19.2: **Comparative Energy Consumption Levels**

Unit: Percentage

Country	Steel Making Route		
	OH	BOF	EAF
U.K.	-	74.2	25.8
U.S.A.	-	60.6	39.4
Germany	1.5	76.9	21.6
Japan	-	68.8	29.7
Italy	-	42.5	57.4
Spain	-	42.3	57.7
Sweden	-	64.0	36.0
India	25.8	47.4	26.6

identified Energy Conservation as one of the major corporate thrust areas in 1987. Consequently guidelines for energy conservation were laid under the Corporate Plan of the company. The Energy conservation plan envisages a 30 per cent reduction in the specific energy consumption level by the year 2004-5 AD. The threefold strategy formulated to achieve this ambitious goal involves—

1. Restructuring of the Organisational Framework;

TABLE 19.3: **Energy Consumption in BOF and Open Cast Methodologies**

Country	BOF	Opencast Technology
U.K.	74.2	86.1
U.S.A.	60.6	85.7
Germany	76.9	93.9
Japan	68.8	95.7
Italy	42.5	96.5
Spain	42.3	95.9
Sweden	64.0	88.7
India	47.4	43.5

2. Formulation of Energy Conservation Plan; and
3. Implementation of energy conservation measures.

Restructuring of the Organisational Framework

Organisational structure both at corporate level as well as plant level was restructured in order to take up energy conservation activities in the real earnest. A three tier organisation for planning, implementation and monitoring of energy conservation measures was evolved:

1. *Steering group*—The steering group on energy headed by the Chairman, SAIL with Managing Director, Director (Finance) and Director (Operations) as members is the highest body which formulates the policy on energy conservation and approves medium term schemes involving relatively larger capital investment.
2. *Corporate level task force on energy*—The Corporate level task force headed by Executive Director (Operations) has representatives from different steel plants and RDCIS. It regularly reviews the performance of energy parameters and also implementation of various energy conservation measures.
3. *Plant level task force on energy*—The plant level task force on energy under the chairmanship of head of works is

responsible for preparation and implementation of the energy conservation plan for each steel plant. It monitors the energy performance of the steel plants on monthly basis.

Apart from this, Energy Management Department was set up in each plant for energy auditing, maintaining the energy facilities and monitoring of energy flow in the plant.

The Energy Conservation Plan

The close nexus between energy and economics of a process necessitated the formulation of energy conservation plan.

The Energy Conservation Plan of SAIL lays out targets to be achieved by systematic and sustained efforts in the following broad areas:

- — operational improvements.
- — equipment improvements.
- — modernisation measures.

Briefly these measures revolve around:

1. Reduction in coal to blast furnace coke ratio.
2. Reduction of coke rate in blast furnaces.
3. Reduction in hot metal to liquid steel ratio.
4. Improvement in metallic yield in steel making.
5. Suppressed gas recovery system for LD converters.
6. Reduction in liquid steel to crude steel ratio.
7. Reduction in petrofuel consumption through increased recovery of byeproduct gases namely coke oven gas.
8. Decrease in specific heat consumption of soaking pits and reheating furnaces.
9. Introduction of waste heat recovery systems in different areas.
10. Elimination of wastages and leakages of steam, compressed air and oxygen.

The plan also quantifies the energy consumption level to be

achieved by each unit of SAIL as a result of implementation of the energy conservation measures (Table 19.4).

TABLE 19.4

Unit: Gcal/tcs

SAIL steel unit	2005 A.D.
Bhilai Steel Plant	6.5
Durgapur Steel Plant	8.0
Rourkela Steel Plant	7.8
Bokaro Steel Unit	7.5
Indian Iron & Steel Company (Burnpur)	7.8

Implementation of Energy Conservation Programme

SAIL had commissioned the expert team from British Steel Corporation under UNDP/UNIDO assisted project for carrying out a detailed energy audit of Bhilai, Bokaro and Rourkela units. Similarly, SAIL had also commissioned expert teams from NKK, Japan under a SAIL-NKK contract for its Durgapur, Rourkela and Burnpur units. The recommendations made by the two teams helped in identifying the potential energy saving areas in SAIL. Thereafter, based on the nature of the scheme, the payback period and the cost involved, the energy conservation schemes to be implemented were determined and classified under:

- Short term measures;
- Medium term measures; and
- Long term measures.

Short Term Measures

The short term measures incur minimal investments and are taken up on a regular basis. These include—

- Elimination of steam, oil and compressed air leakages.

— Improved house-keeping.
— Maintenance of proper air-fuel ratio in reheating furnaces.
— Adherence to optimal thermal regimes, etc.

Medium Term Measures

The medium term measures include among others installation of microprocessor controlled combustion systems, introduction of variable speed drives, hydrojet cleaning of oven doors. Annexure gives the medium term measures that have already been implemented in the integrated steel units, the list is indicative but not exhaustive.

Long Term Measures

The long term measures include the schemes taken up as a part of technology upgradation and modernisation programme such as partial briquetting of coal charge, stamp charging in coke ovens, coal dust injection in blast furnaces, replacement of open-hearth furnaces by basic oxygen furnaces, introduction of bell-less top in blast furnaces, installation of combined cycle power plant. Some of these measures are already being implemented across the company.

SAIL has also introduced a system of setting up shopwise targets of energy parameters for different shops in each steel plant alongwith the target for overall energy consumption. The energy management personnel closely interact with operational departments to determine the reasons for variance from targets. This analysis helps in evolving the corrective measures to be taken for achieving the targets.

Apart from the technical aspects, the culture of an organisation has a marked bearing on the energy conservation in a steel plant. Realising the significance of human factor, SAIL in its pursuit to conserve energy has made concerted efforts in educating and training its employees through workshops, classroom lectures, banners, posters, etc. This has immensely helped in generating energy consciousness in the entire workforce of SAIL.

It is the result of implementation of the aforementioned energy conservation measures that the energy consumption level in SAIL has decreased by 23 per cent from 1986-87 to 1994-95.

Future Prospects

There are a number of new and improved energy saving technologies which are technically established but often display low levels of investment efficiency. However, these can be examined for their technoeconomic feasibility w.r.t. SAIL steel units. Some of these technologies are discussed below.

Coke Dry Quenching

The coke extracted from the ovens is at very high temperature. In the conventional system, it is cooled down by spraying water on it. Dry quenching of coke helps in extracting the sensible heat of the high temperature coke and converts it to high pressure steam which can be further used to generate power.

Top Pressure Recovery Turbine

The modern blast furnaces are high capacity furnaces. These furnaces operate at high top pressure. The high top pressure of the gas is exploited in the gas expansion turbines to generate power.

Natural Gas Injection

Use of natural gas in blast furnaces alongwith oxygen is a proven technology for maximising the productivity of the furnace and decreasing its coke consumption.

Coal Bed Methane Gas

The possibility of recovering coal bed methane gas from the eastern coal fields is being examined at the national level. In case the project materialises SAIL can consider using coal bed methane gas as a fuel injectant in the blast furnaces to cut down on coke consumption of the furnaces.

Alternate Routes of Iron-making

The need for an alternative iron-making technology arises out of the demand to conserve the depleting resources of good quality coking coal. In view of the success of Corex technology in the process of iron making, SAIL is considering the development of an indigenous concept of adoption of the imported technology.

SAIL has also signed a memorandum of understanding with AMET for imbibing Russian technology in the Romelt process of iron making. It is a simple, one step process for direct iron smelting. This process utilize simple coal fines as both the fuel and the reductant. It is also capable of smelting wide range of ores and metallurgical waste materials.

Conclusion

Although SAIL has achieved a remarkable reduction in its energy consumption level by adopting energy saving measures, but it still has a long way to go. Through continued efforts for energy conservation in the existing facilities as well as through modernisation of facilities, it is planned to further accelerate the energy conservation drive in SAIL.

ANNEXURE

ENERGY CONSERVATION SCHEMES

Some of the energy conservation schemes that have been taken up in SAIL steel plants are:

1. Monitoring of maximum demand of electrical power: BSP
2. Installation of modified water cooled skids in reheating furnace No. 1 and 3 of Merchant Mill: BSP
3. Modified Ladle Heating Stand for SMS-1: BSP
4. Insulation of cold blast main for blast furnaces: BSP
5. Time switches for switching off street lights: BSP
6. Micro-processor based controller in reheating furnaces of Wire Rod Mill: BSP
7. Soft start and pulsar AC variable speed drive for hot saw mill motor of Rail and Structural Mill: BSP
8. Use of ceramic fibre lining in Annealing Furnaces of CRM-1: BSL
9. Automatic street lighting on-off devices in township: BSL
10. Conversion of high pressure mercury vapour lamps to high pressure sodium vapour lamps: BSL
11. Oxygen enrichment of cold blast, BF4: BSL
12. On line steam leakage plugging: BSL
13. Double skid insulation in reheating furnaces: RSP
14. Thermal insulation of fuel oil tanks: RSP
15. Ceramic fibre sealing in hood annealing furnaces: RSP
16. Insulation of fibre glass translucent sheets for roof tops in mills area: RSP
17. High emissivity coating in electric sheet mill furnace: RSP
18. HYSIL brick lining in soaking pits: RSP
19. High emissivity coating in sleeper plant reheating furnace: DSP
20. High emissivity application in soaking pit No. 3: DSP
21. Electrical tape heating in SMS area: DSP
22. Installation of booster for coke oven gas at sinter plant: DSP

23. Micro-processor based control system for soaking pits: IISCO
24. Ladle drying covers: IISCO
25. Dynamic reactive power compensation for Arc Furnace operation: ASP
26. Reactive Power Compensation: DSP
27. Reactive Power Compensation: RSP
28. 220 KV power supply for DSP and ASP
29. Supervisory Load Control Centres at DSP, BSL, RSP and Calcutta for optimisation of captive power vis-a-vis import from utility.

Key

BSP - Bhilai Steel Plant
DSP - Durgapur Steel Plant
RSP - Rourkela Steel Plant
BSL - Bokaro Steel Plant
IISCO- Indian Iron & Steel Company, Burnpur
ASP - Alloy Steel Plant

TWENTY

ENERGY CONSERVATION IN CAPTIVE POWER PLANT AT HINDALCO

AJAY SRIVASTAVA

Introduction

Renusagar is a coal based thermal captive power plant of 350 MW capacity of Hindalco Industries Limited. It has 5 T.G. sets. The first 2 units were commissioned in 1967-68, Units No. 3 and 4 in 1981-83, whereas Unit No. 5 was commissioned in 1989.

Plant Load Factor

Renusagar has achieved excellent performance track record. It has consistently achieved high Plant Load Factor (PLF) in the range of 80-95 per cent right from its inception. The PLF for the year 1994-95 was 94.29 per cent.

Plant Availability Factor

During the last decade, everyone involved in the energy sector, whether industry captains or policy makers, has discussed at length the importance of high Plant Load Factor. However, what should have really gained significance, is the Plant Availability Factor (PAF). Annual Plant Availability Factor is the measure of the percentage of time, energy generating machinery was available for power production during the year, considering its outage for planned and forced/breakdown maintenance. It would be pertinent to note that the Plant Availability Factor for Renusagar has been in the range to 85-96 per cent.

It may be emphasized here that there are no short-cuts to success and that the high PAF, that has been achieved at Renusagar, is a result of concerted efforts and strict implementation of quality control measures, which have improved the equipment reliability and has kept outages due to break-downs to the barest minimum. The methodology of rolling maintenance plan and the conceptual approach by the various maintenance departments concerned, has paid rich dividends to the organization in curtailing maintenance time.

Comprehensive and Detailed Planning

Comprehensive overhauling and maintenance rolling plan, suitably phased and coordinated with spares/consumables procurement and support manpower arrangement, have been found to be effective. Knowledge Integration Programme emerging from Inter-unit visits and breakdown analysis by the technical group, identifying the cause and spelling out of an action plan coupled with meticulous follow-up action, have been found to be extremely beneficial by the power plant division.

The maintenance procedures were broadly on the guidelines, mentioned in the manufacturer's, instructions manuals, but the emphasis on superior workmanship and quality control has culminated in the development of maintenance culture, where job is done "first time right", and simultaneously, innovative efforts for continuous improvement are encouraged.

In view of the experience gained at Renusagar, it is recommended that when the short and long term action plans are discussed and focus is made on managerial input, emphasis should be laid on:

- (i) Strategic rolling maintenance plan,
- (ii) Breakdown analysis and action plan to avoid recurrence,
- (iii) Review of quality assurance system, and
- (iv) Incentive schemes for innovative ideas and suggestions for continuous improvement.

Training of Personnel

Power industry being capital intensive, mal-operation results in enormous financial loss not only in equipment replacement, but also in loss of production. As such, Renusagar has laid emphasis on training and skills development of its personnel. For the graduate and diploma engineers, induction level training has been formulated for imparting knowledge on the boiler, turbine, pumps, fans, compressors, motors, switchgears, etc., through classroom lectures, specially designed models, workshop, techniques and exposure to on job planned training. Besides the induction level training, refresher courses are held for the experienced hands periodically. Workshops and seminars are arranged in-house to familiarize the technical personnel of the latest trends and developments in various fields. To improve the confidence and response time, under the emergent conditions, a structured course on upset conditions has been held for all operation personnel and surprise drills are held occasionally. Realising the paramount importance of attitudinal change, courses on behavioural sciences are held for HOD's and executives, supervisory development programmes for the shop floor personnel and workers development programmes for the work-force in general.

It is recommended that in the mid-term action plan, development of in-house training centre at various power plants for information dissemination, knowledge integration, refresher courses and skills development should be brought into focus. This shall be the real boon for the technical human resource development. Even the long term requirement of attitudinal change, can be speeded up through behavioural sciences course, to be conducted for the different levels of personnel.

Energy Conservation Measures

At Renusagar, station auxiliary consumption has been given due weightage right from the technical evaluation of the equipment procurement proposal. Over-sizing of the main equipment auxiliary and the common services has been consciously avoided.

To carry out systematic work on energy conservation, a technical cell was formed about 12 years ago. It examined the areas threadbare and developed systems for close monitoring. To cross-check the measures taken, an independent study was assigned to the National Productivity Council in 1985. The specific energy conservation measures, taken at Renusagar, are:

1. Review of boiler inter-locking circuit and its modification.
2. Discontinuing the practice of:

   (i) Keeping standby boiler in warmed up condition, and
   (ii) Keeping standby pulverizer in floating condition.

3. Energy audit of common services and fixation of norms vis-a-vis design data and daily/shift-wise check sheets covering the areas of:

   (i) Coal crushing and conveying,
   (ii) Ash handling and disposal,
   (iii) Make up water pumps operation,
   (iv) Compressed air for service and instrumentation.

4. Pumping power conservation by:

   (i) Converting open circuit systems to closed circuit,
   (ii) Developing system for trapping ash dam seepage water and reusing the same,
   (iii) Replacement of over-size pumps by right sizing.

5. Lighting power conservation by:

   (i) Modification and combination of circuits,
   (ii) Replacement of inefficient luminaries,
   (iii) Use of transparent roof sheets in sheds.

6. Welding power conservation by utilizing 'energy saver' device.
7. Introduction of periodic internal technical audit and

implementation of action plans emerging from the same.

Oil Conservation

At Renusagar, HSD/LSD is used only for:

(i) Boiler startup,
(ii) Boiler shutdown,
(iii) Cutting in or out of a pulverizer, and
(iv) Flame instability during grid disturbance or use of inferior wet coal.

During early 80's, the oil consumption had an annual average varying from 1 to 2 ml. per kwh generation.

The technical cell made an indepth analysis for the reasons for oil consumption. It considered the optimum size of the oil gun tips, minimum oil pressure and flow, so as to curtail excessive firing of oil. Simultaneously, norms were fixed in terms of number of igniters and oil guns required for specific time in the various activities. Awareness programme was arranged for the panel engineers, who were made specifically responsible for the oil consumption in their boiler and in their shift. The practice of increasing generation by supplementing oil support was discontinued as a policy. This sort of conceptual approach brought down the oil consumption to consistently less than 1 ml./kwh and has stabilized in the last 3 consecutive years at 0.67 ml./kwh generation.

Coal Conservation and Fuel Cost

Much before the concept of having super power stations at the coal pit head bcame a fad, Renusagar was conceived and installed at mere 7.5 kms. from the Jhingurdah coal mines of Singrauli coal belt beside the Rihand lake in 1967.

When the coal supply from the then NCDÇ was negotiated, Renusagar had insisted on installation of stone picking conveyors at the mine end, so as to avoid transportation of non-carbonious material to the power house. Though the arrangement worked initially, inconsistency crept in and Renusagar had to install stone picking arrangement at the receiving end (though at a smaller scale).

In the national perspective, to contain the expenditure of diesel for coal transportation and to maintain its own coal transportation system, two 7.5 kms. long aerial ropeways have been installed, the first of which was commissioned in 1968. Cost of coal transportation by ropeway is almost half of road transportation cost.

Coal stacking procedures have been designed in such a manner that even during monsoon, feeding of moist and wet coal is extremely rare, and this has enabled the organization to minimize HSD support for furnace flame stability during the monsoon period.

For controlling handling loss, Renusagar has installed Chemjet System, which has controlled loss of fine coal particles at coal unloading, feeding and transfer points.

Materials Management

As a policy, Renusagar procures essential spares along with the main equipments. It interacts with the equipment manufacturer to ascertain the spares requirement for 3 years subsequent to commissioning. Based on the feed-back of the manufacturer and its own experience, particular spare and its quantity is arrived at. On the basis of this exercise, procurement of essential spares are made.

Renusagar concurs with the views that insurance and vital critical spares, the availability of which is vital for the power plant, should be stocked as a policy. However, in case of both critical and non-critical spares, the consumption pattern has to be established to exercise judicious control. Though the market and the infrastructure do not permit implementation of 'just in time' (JIT) concept, vendor development and evaluation technique can effectively contribute towards this goal.

While the technical wing, specially the maintenance department, although advocates 100 per cent service factor, blockage of capital in inventory leads to higher interest and therefore power generation cost. So as to nip in the bud, Renusagar has established an Inventory Control Cell, which scans all purchase requisitions and is following Multi Unit Selective Inventory Control (MUSIC 3D) system.

While discussing the long-term component of the action plan, this point could come into focus, because several power houses remain idle for want of essential spares and ironically, there are several spares, which the power plant had procured more than a decade ago and have never been used. Such an anomaly can be overcome by formulation of a materials management policy and adoption of simple techniques on the lines of Renusagar's Inventory Control Cell.

Conclusion

Despite the fact that Renusagar is relatively small 350 MW captive power plant with 5 units, the management systems, developed here and the excellent results achieved, should inspire the power industry to interact for information dissemination; and after rational analysis, fix targets along with time-bound action plan and monitoring system. What Renusagar has achieved consistently is impressive and worth emulating. It attributes its success to introduction of modern management techniques along with development of skills of its human resource. It may be submitted with all humility that what Renusagar has done at a small scale, can be achieved at the macro level by the nation through meaningful decisions in the 'National Workshop on Energy Conservation'.

TWENTY-ONE

ENERGY CONSERVATION IN SUGAR INDUSTRY

PALANI G. PERIASAMY

Sugar industry by nature is bestowed with a crop which has abundant potential for renewable energy. The conservation of energy resources will not only make available extra energy for other uses but also reduce the cost of energy at different stages of manufacture in any industry. It is in this context we should look upon new avenues for efficient use of energy taking into account the prevailing practice without any additional expenditure. The raw material, sugar cane, yields a series of by-products each of which has a special use in the industry. The bagasse is used as fuel for boiler apart from other uses as raw material in paper, boards etc., The trash can be used as a biomass fuel for generation of power, the filter cake, which can be used as a fertilizer on gasification, could produce energy also.

Plan of Action Necessary to Effect Energy Conservation

To look at the short term plan with the present day context we should subject ourselves in the sugar industry to the energy audit and plug the drain wherever possible. This will go a long way in identifying and locating the areas where improvement can be made in the existing set-up. On a medium term plan of action we should improve the performance of the industry by modernisation and rehabilitation with particular reference to energy. For instance, we can change the low pressure boiler to high pressure boiler and derive benefit. On a long term basis the industry can put up new projects that are coming up with a concept of co-generation as a energy saving device as well as to generate surplus power for export for other end users. Under this category we are putting up a modern sugar plant with a co-generation plant of 15 MW for captive use and for export of power to the grid which is to be commissioned shortly.

Possibility of Energy Conservation

We should explore the possibility of energy conservation in different areas in the sugar industry, such as the following:

(i) Study the energy consumption and to reduce the same to the optimum level by the best possible prime movers available.
(ii) Efficient generation and use of steam and effective utilization of the heating surfaces.
(iii) Continuous operation of processes, wherever possible, and introduction of techniques like continuous pan boiling.
(iv) Minimising the energy consumption in centrifugals by introduction of improved designs with recycling (energy saving) drive mechanism.
(v) Saving water and power consumption by use of efficient condensing system.
(vi) Modernisation of the industry by use of the latest technological development and innovations.

Energy Consumption Data

Further in the sugar industry there is no data compilation available on the consumption pattern and if this is analysed it will throw more light and we should strive hard to achieve the lowest energy cost per unit sugar production. We should aim at a consumption level of 15/16 KW hr per unit sugar.

Conclusion

By adopting above measures contemplated in 418 existing sugar factories it may be possible to produce additional power equivalent of around 2,000 MW installed capacity. A national level Technical Sub Committee under the aegis of Indian Sugar Mills Association, National Federation of Co-operative Sugar Factories and Sugar Technologists Association of India in co-ordination with State and Central Governments should give a lead to the industry.

TWENTY-TWO

RECOMMENDATIONS AND ACTION PLAN

A 2-Day National Workshop on Energy Conservation was jointly organised by The Rajiv Gandhi Institute for Contemporary Studies (Rajiv Gandhi Foundation) and The Institution of Engineers (India) on September 8-9, 1995 in New Delhi. The participants at the Workshop included policy makers, industrialists, scientists, economists and energy conservation experts. Major recommendations and the action plan developed at this National Workshop are as follows:

RECOMMENDATIONS

The following recommendations emerged:

1. The fiscal and physical targets in the energy conservation sector laid down in the 8th Five Year Plan are not likely to be achieved. This was a matter of concern and immediate action was required at the national level to develop a strategy to initiate appropriate and relevant energy conservation programme in the country.
2. As an initial step, a non-statutory body of professional experts may be set up to identify the areas for energy conservation in the country and also to develop appropriate fiscal incentives and legislative measures that will bring around the required results.

   An important area for consideration of the body would be the mechanism of energy audit in large energy consuming industries, whether through government energy auditors or through an independent forum of energy auditors.

3. Subsequently, a statutory autonomous body at the centre would be necessary to decide about incentives and disincentives; and to have necessary administrative and legislative authority.
4. The autonomous body may effectively implement energy conservation programme through state nodal agencies and professional bodies with built-in flexibility of operation.
5. Energy conservation policy must be developed by the government with time bound targets and clearly defined thrust areas.
6. An action plan needs be developed defining short term, medium term and long term measures and the strategy to be followed for attaining identified targets.

ACTION PLAN

The following Action Plan was adopted:

Preamble

The energy scene in the country is of grave concern, and all out effort is necessary to achieve installation of additional energy capacities to support economic development target in the country. Achievement in the power sector is far short of the plan target, and foreign investment is not forthcoming at a pace anticipated earlier. Under these circumstances, the need for energy conservation and energy use efficiency improvement become relevant. Rationalisation in production and use of energy will be an effective route for attaining the desired goal.

Modest initiatives of the government, through PCRA and EMC, and the efforts of the industry, mainly large scale, have achieved a breakthrough. It is now necessary to consolidate on the efforts already made in the industrial sector and to launch initiatives in agriculture, transport and household sectors to save energy in perceptible terms.

The following Action Plan emerged:

I. Objective

The objective of the action plan is to effect energy conservation to attain savings of equivalent of 5,000 MW of installed generating capacity and 6 mt of oil by the year 2002 (The target is the same as kept for VIII Plan); and to develop an effective monitoring system for collection, collation and compilation of these savings.

II. Target Group

Target group shall include

(i) Energy consuming sector in industrial, domestic, agricultural and transport activities; and

(ii) Energy producing sector.

III. Approach

The approach of the action plan for effective energy conservation measure in the country requires following two elements:

(i) *Fiscal Incentives* — The government shall have to provide fiscal incentives linked to energy savings and tax concessions, rather than subsidies;

(ii) *Legislative Measures* — The government shall have to develop an Energy Conservation Act and ensure its strict implementation. (A persuasive approach of awareness creation and education about energy conservation measures may lead to better acceptability of the act)

The risk financing of the energy conservation technology shall be a major concern of the government.

The present day subsidised energy services need to be replaced by schemes that encourage energy efficiency and have the same beneficial results. Wherever subsidies are necessary they should be very specific in their objective and of short term. They may need to form part of an evolving policy, with successive short term schemes directed at promoting energy efficiency and encouraging conservation. The legislative measures should be more in terms of rationalising the use of energy in different applications. The law needs to provide measures for factories, machinery, equipment, buildings and services. Mandatory standards for machines and equipment need to be evolved.

IV. Strategy

A four-pronged strategy needs to be adopted with specific time bound programme. The approach has to be pragmatic. Shorter time period result-oriented programme should call for lower level of technology interventions and lower financial investments. The four-pronged conservation approach shall be as follows:

(i) *Better house keeping* which may lead to 5 to 10% of energy saving, on an average, in all the four sectors of use. Such an approach can be followed by inculcating the habit of maintaining systems as per the laid down norms. This shall be a low or no investment approach, but shall be universally applicable/acceptable and affordable in every sector.

(ii) *Increased efficiency of existing systems* mainly retrofitting the production units/equipment with more efficient energy use sub-systems which may result in saving, on an average, of 10% and over at a moderate investment level.

(iii) *New technologies* that call for introduction of state-of-the-art machines, new processes, etc which may help in energy saving of 25% and over, on an average. Such an option is highly cost intensive.

(iv) *New Sources of Energy*, mainly renewable in nature, may enable a saving of 50-80%. This intervention shall call for change in use pattern and attitudinal change in the user.

V. Time Frame

The short-term measures would be in terms of improvements in operational measures and the long-term measures would be in terms of strategic improvements and call for large investments. Thus, the following 3-tier time bound action plan is suggested:

Short term measures:	1995-1997 (end of VIII Five Year Plan)
Medium term measures:	Upto 2002 (end of IX Five Year Plan)
Long term measures:	By 2007 and beyond (end of X Five Year Plan)

(i) Short-Term Measures

These measures shall require intensive efforts to promote the following:

(i) Better housekeeping; and
(ii) Increased efficiency of existing systems.

During this short-term phase, initiatives may also be launched to study the options of new technologies and new energy sources.

(ii) Medium Term Measures

These shall include continuation of activities launched in the short-term, on which the government spending will gradually decrease; and to promote introduction use of new technologies in terms of state-of-the-art machines and new processes which, in other words, will be justified because of global industrial competition.
Whereas investments in this phase by the government would decrease, the institutional finance requirement would increase.
The target of energy conservation for the 8th Five Year Plan, set by the government, for 5-year period of 1992-97 has been adopted for 1997-2002, to be achieved in 2002 under medium term of the Action Plan.

(iii) Long Term Measures

These need futuristic biological and bio-technological applications and require R&D support.

VI. Funds Required

Short term measures:	Plan allocation of Rs. 1,000 crores
Medium term measures:	Plan allocation of Rs. 1,000 crores and institutional finance of Rs. 6 to 10,000 crores
Long term measures:	To be financed by energy savings due to actions in the short term and medium term.

Activities under short term measures may be launched such that allocation made in the VIII Five Year Plan, at Rs. 1,000 crores, is effectively utilised to create the necessary Statutory Independent Authority for Energy Conservation at the centre with powers to frame and enact subordinate legislative steps; and corresponding nodal agencies in the states with financial support from the proposed Statutory Independent Authority (existing institutions like PCRA and EMC to become a part of the Statutory Independent Authority); to support awareness creation; to provide fiscal incentives to promote good housekeeping and efficiency improvement of existing systems; and to support initiatives that may bear fruit during medium term and long term phases.

During the medium term phase, allocation of Rs. 1,000 crores may be made also during IX Five Year plan to support awareness creation; to provide fiscal incentive on a sliding scale, and to support R&D. The institutional finance required may be taken directly in terms of the money expected to be saved by savings of power generation or oil import. The target of 5,000 MW would have required Rs. 20,000 crores of investment and import of 6 million tons would have required about Rs. 4,000 crores. The institutional finance to the tune of Rs. 24,000 crores would have been required for additional capacities. It is estimated that availability of Rs. 6-10,000 crores would bring about the necessary energy savings to offset additional capacities.

During the long term phase efforts need be made to promote users to suitably invest out of the funds generated by them by savings in fuel bills due to introduction of high efficiency energy conversion equipment during the 12-year period upto 2007.

VII. Infrastructure

A Statutory Independent Authority for energy conservation needs to be set up which has all the legislative, administrative and financial powers. Institutions like PCRA and EMC, presently involved in energy conservation, form strong implementing arms. Corresponding nodal agencies in States may be identified/set up and initially supported through funds from the Centre.

Financial allocations as suggested earlier shall be necessary for effective action.

VIII. Immediate Actions

Following activities may be taken up on priority without waiting for formal infrastructure creation (and through already existing mechanism):

1. Accelerated depreciation provisions for energy efficiency equipment may be expanded so that the rate of depreciation for such equipment is increased from 50 per cent to 100 per cent in line with the existing provisions for the pollution control equipment.
2. A forum of energy auditors, who are professional experts, be set up. The forum may develop into an apex body, like The Institution of Chartered Accountants for financial audit, and may lay down norms for the energy auditors.
3. Base line data should be gathered for different categories of industries to decide on the approach for energy conservation. Parallel action in different sectors of activities may be initiated. Priority may be given to the following large energy consumers: (i) steel industry (ii) power generation sector (iii) aluminium industry (iv) paper and pulp industry and (v) textiles industry. Efforts must also be made to collect

base line data in clusters of small scale industries.

4. Energy consumption norms should be developed for energy intensive industry.
5. Various energy using devices may be identified for energy conservation and standards prepared for the Bureau of Indian Standards to implement.
6. Manufacturing industry may be encouraged to adopt energy labelling.
7. Quality control at the manufacturing stage of energy equipment may be taken up on priority. Phasing out of energy inefficient equipment and product manufacturing facilities should be accelerated.
8. Education and training material aimed at awareness creation and skills building may be prepared. Necessary training courses and awareness creation compaigns may be launched. A mechanism for monitoring energy conservation programme may be evolved to keep an eye on the energy conservation efforts.
9. Commercial consultancy services may be promoted to expedite energy conservation movement as their interfacing with the beneficiary is always for commercial reasons.
10. Cogeneration should be promoted as a measure of energy conservation.

INDEX